In each stroke, in each color, discover the power of creativity that lives within you. Let your imagination soar and transform each page of this book into a unique masterpiece.

Luck Rocha
2024

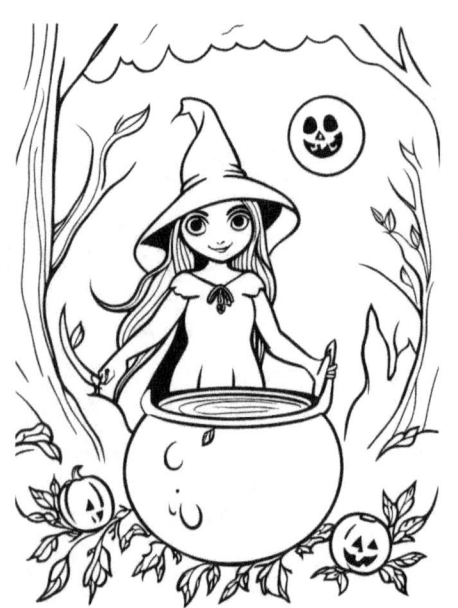 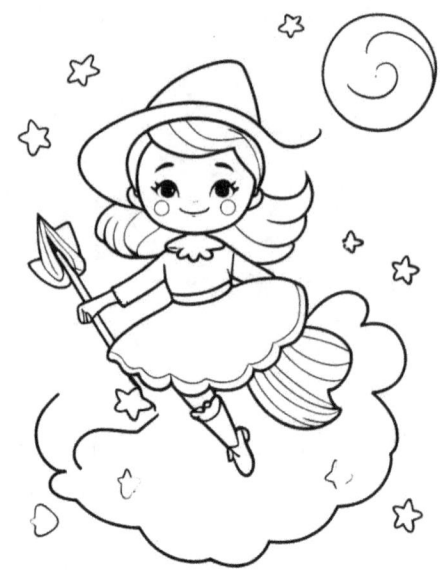

This Book Belongs to:

_____

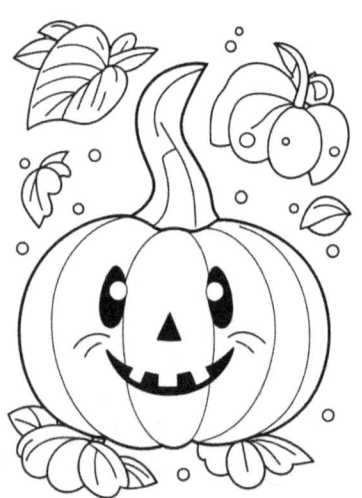 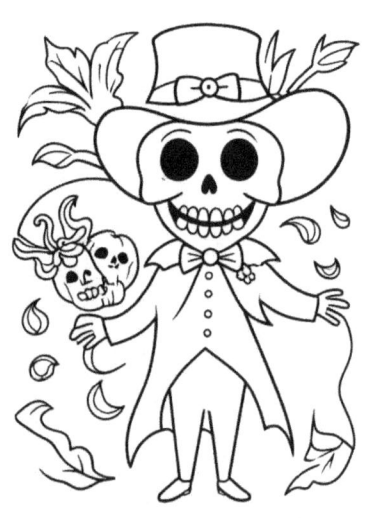

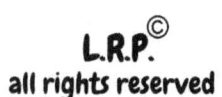

ALL RIGHTS RESERVED©
2024

No part of this publication may be reproduced, distributed, or transmitted in any form or by any means, including photocopying, recording, or other electronic or mechanical methods, without the prior written permission of the publisher, except for brief quotations incorporated in critical reviews and other specific noncommercial uses. Any unauthorized replica of this work is prohibited.

L.R.P.©
Luck Rocha publications

Test Color Page

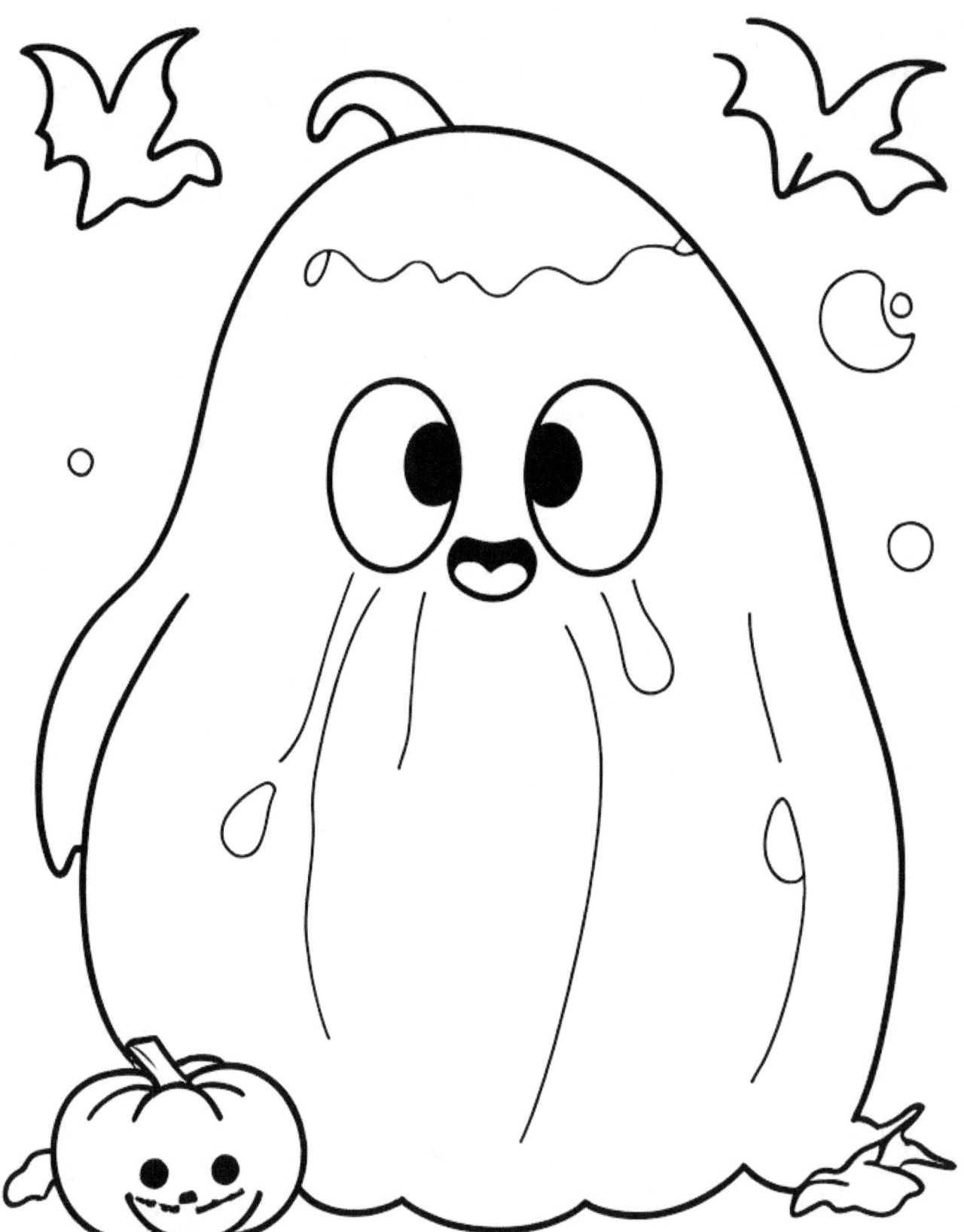

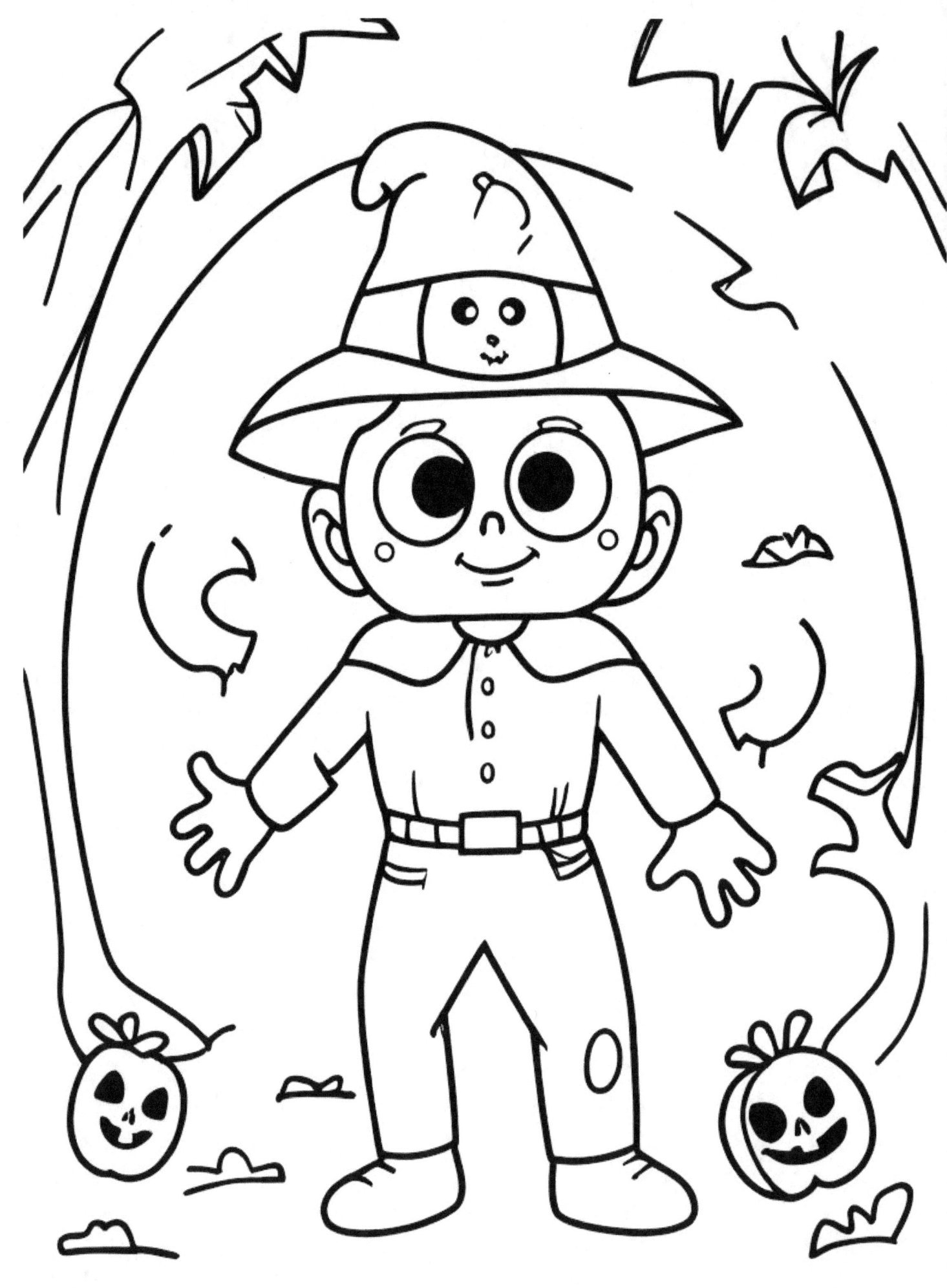

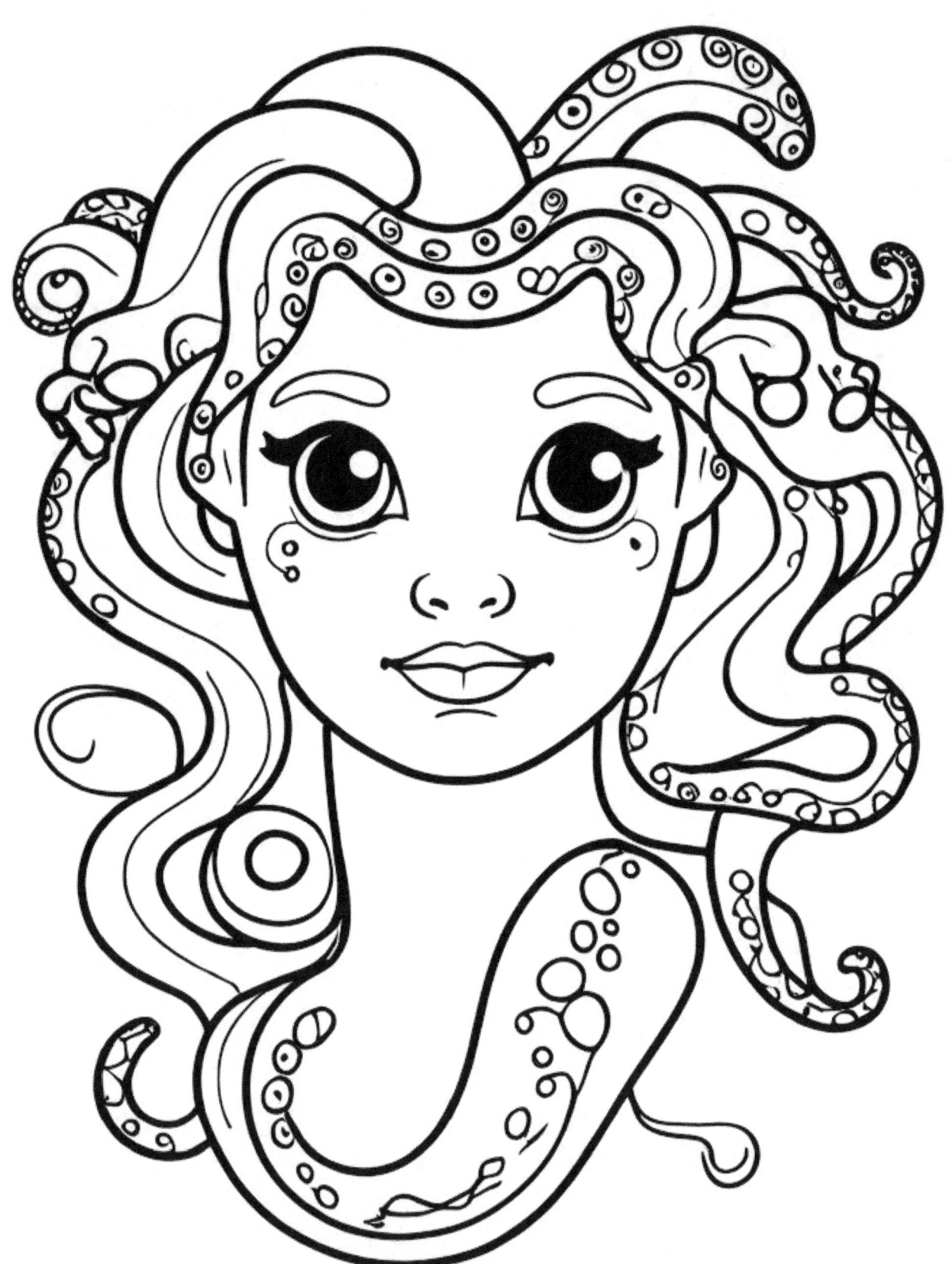

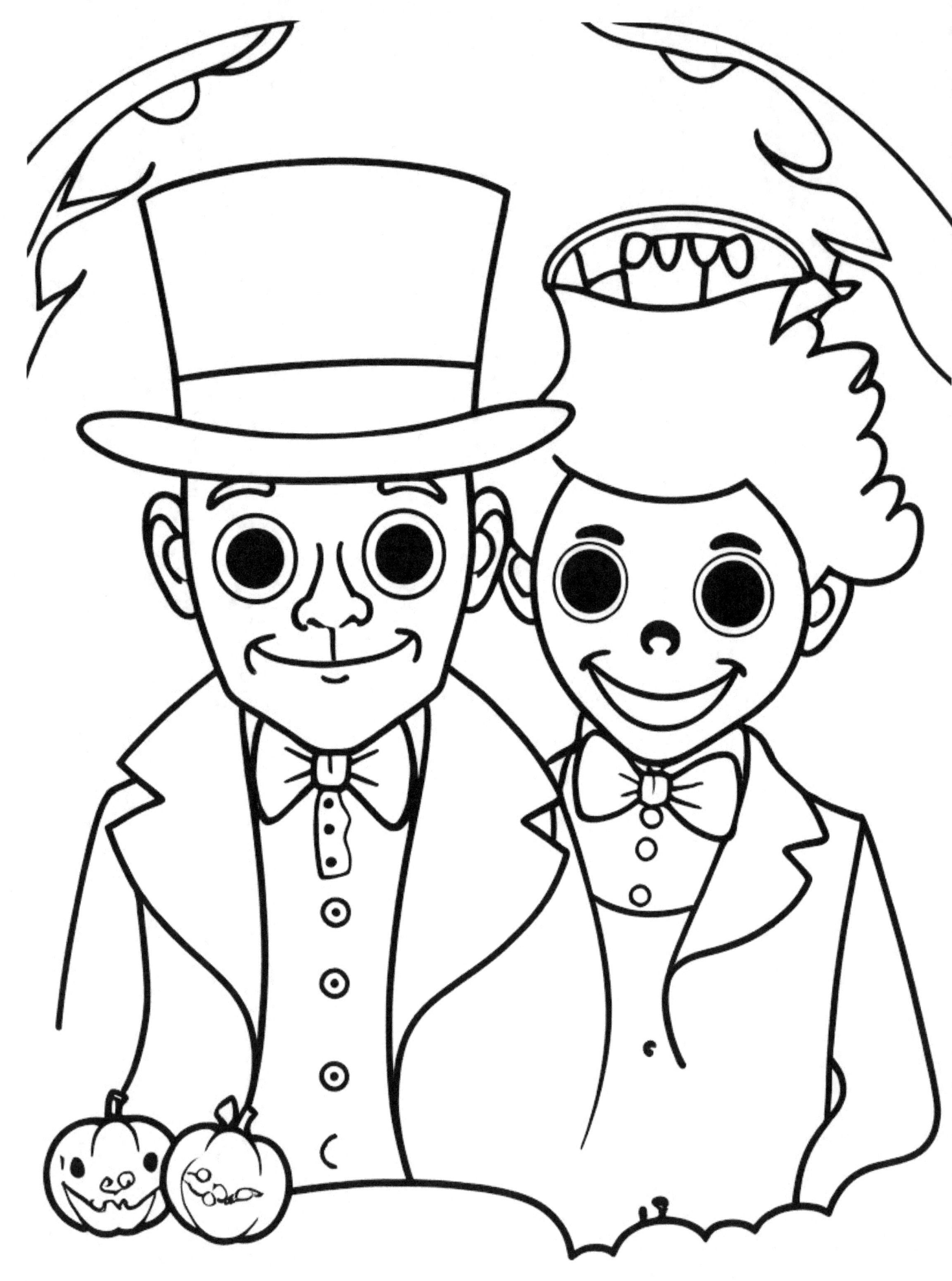

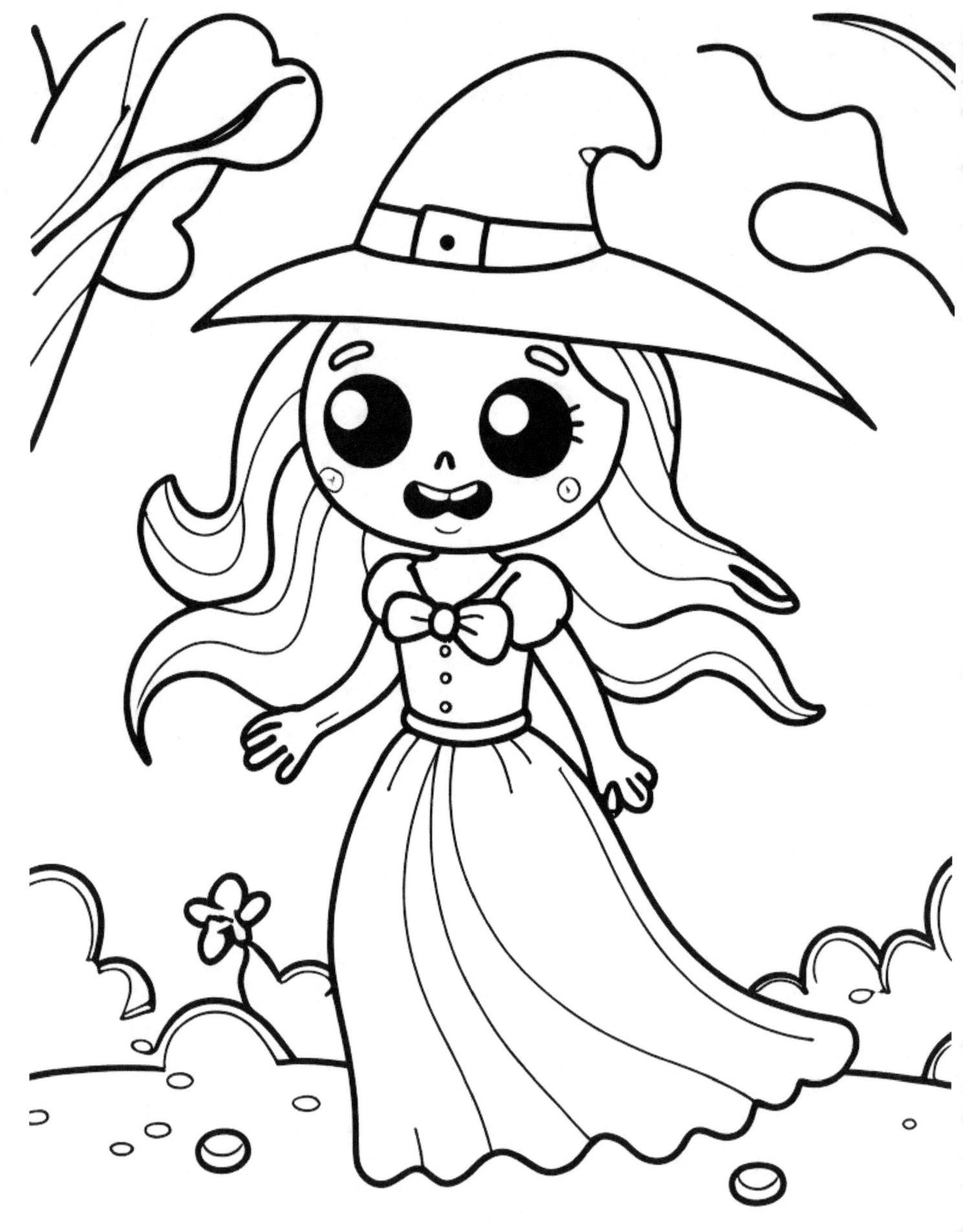

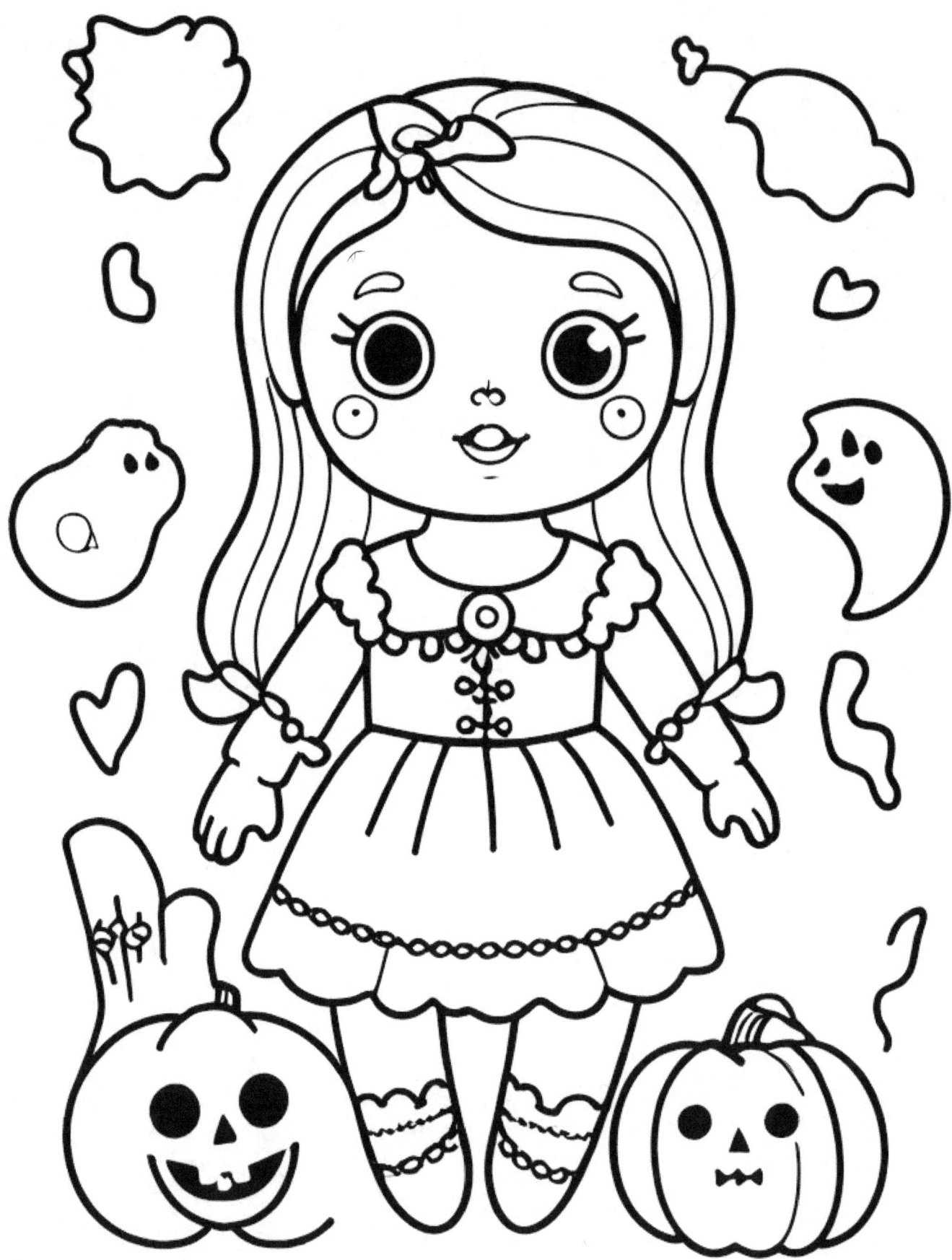

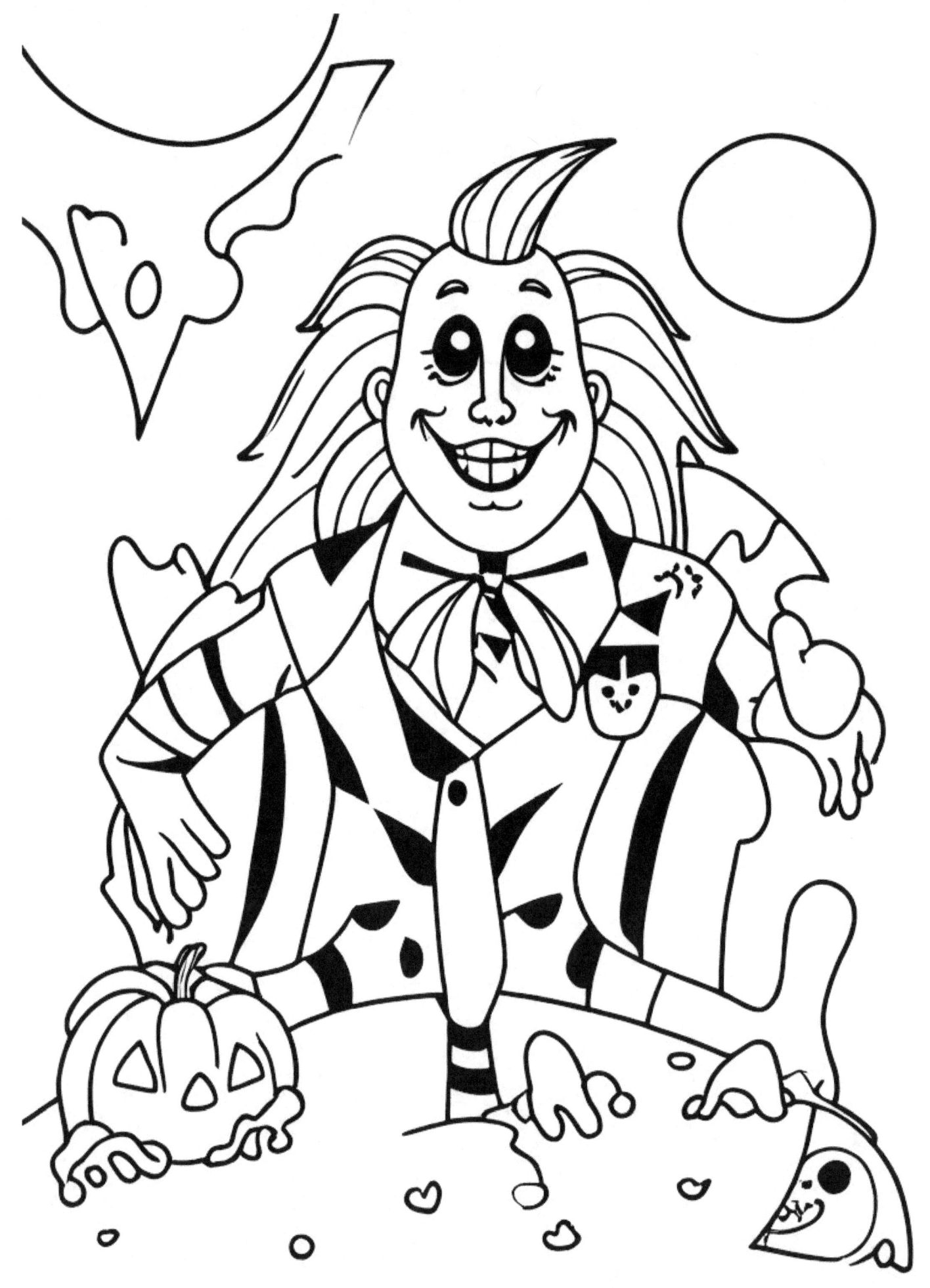

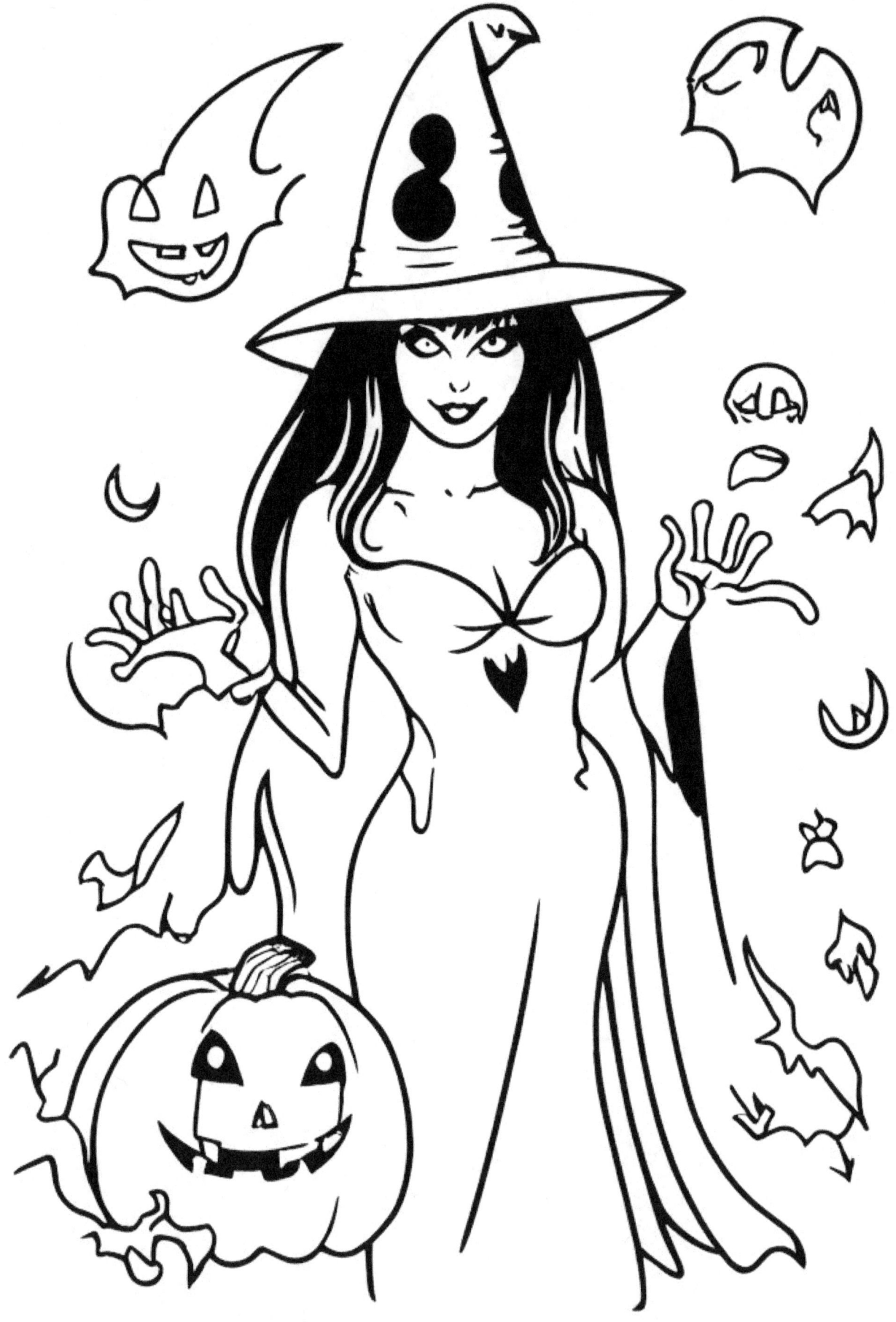

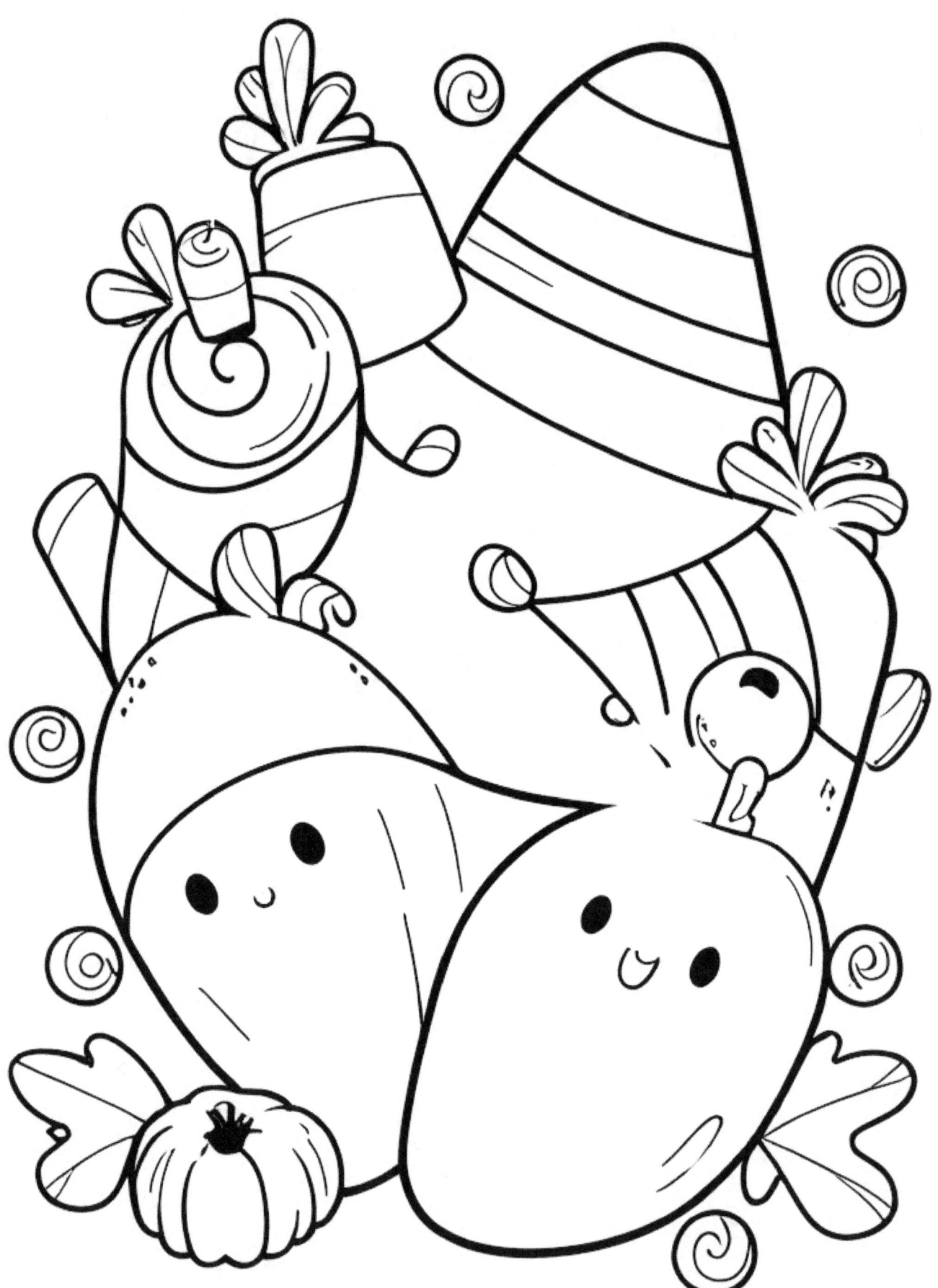

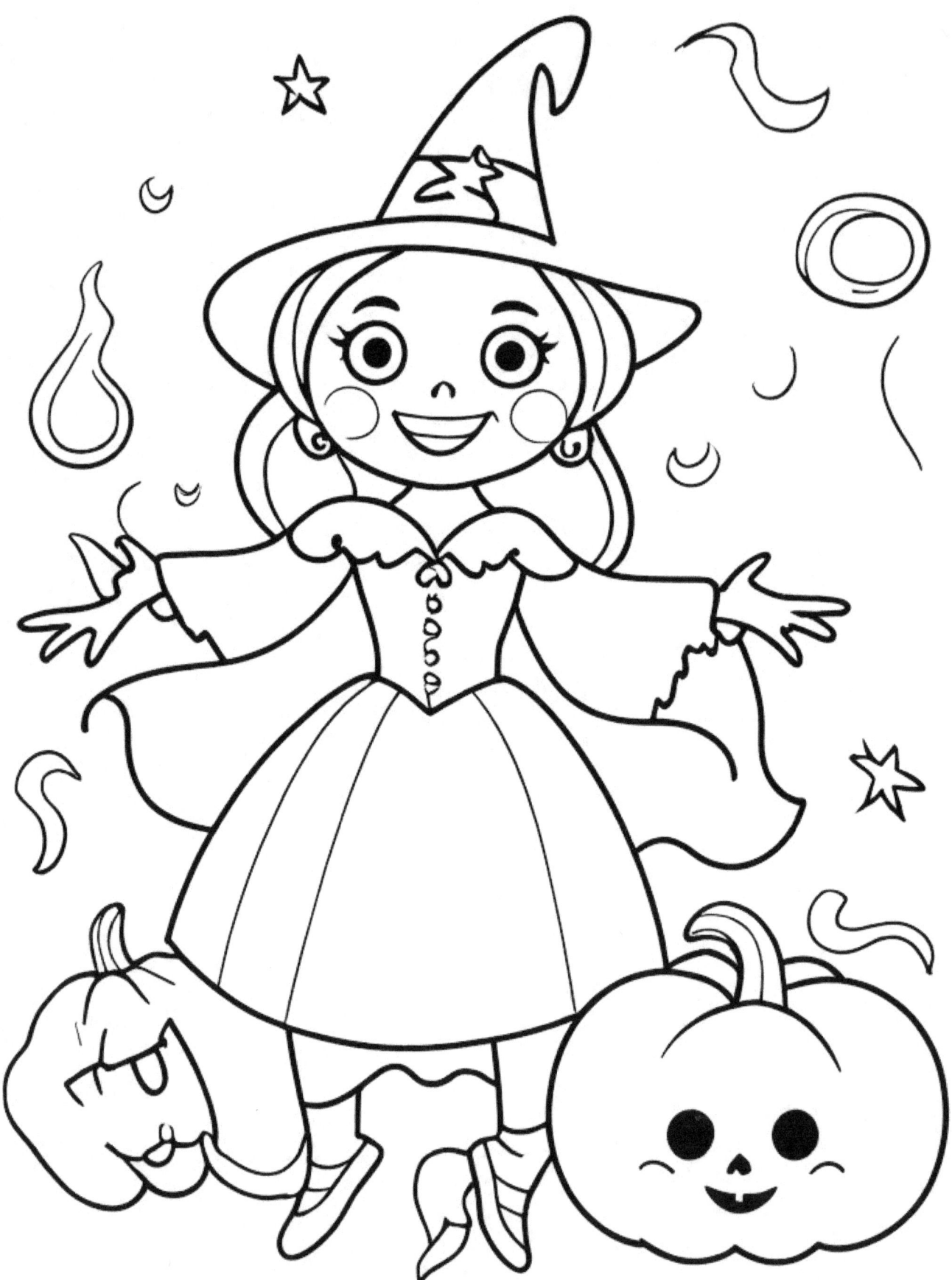

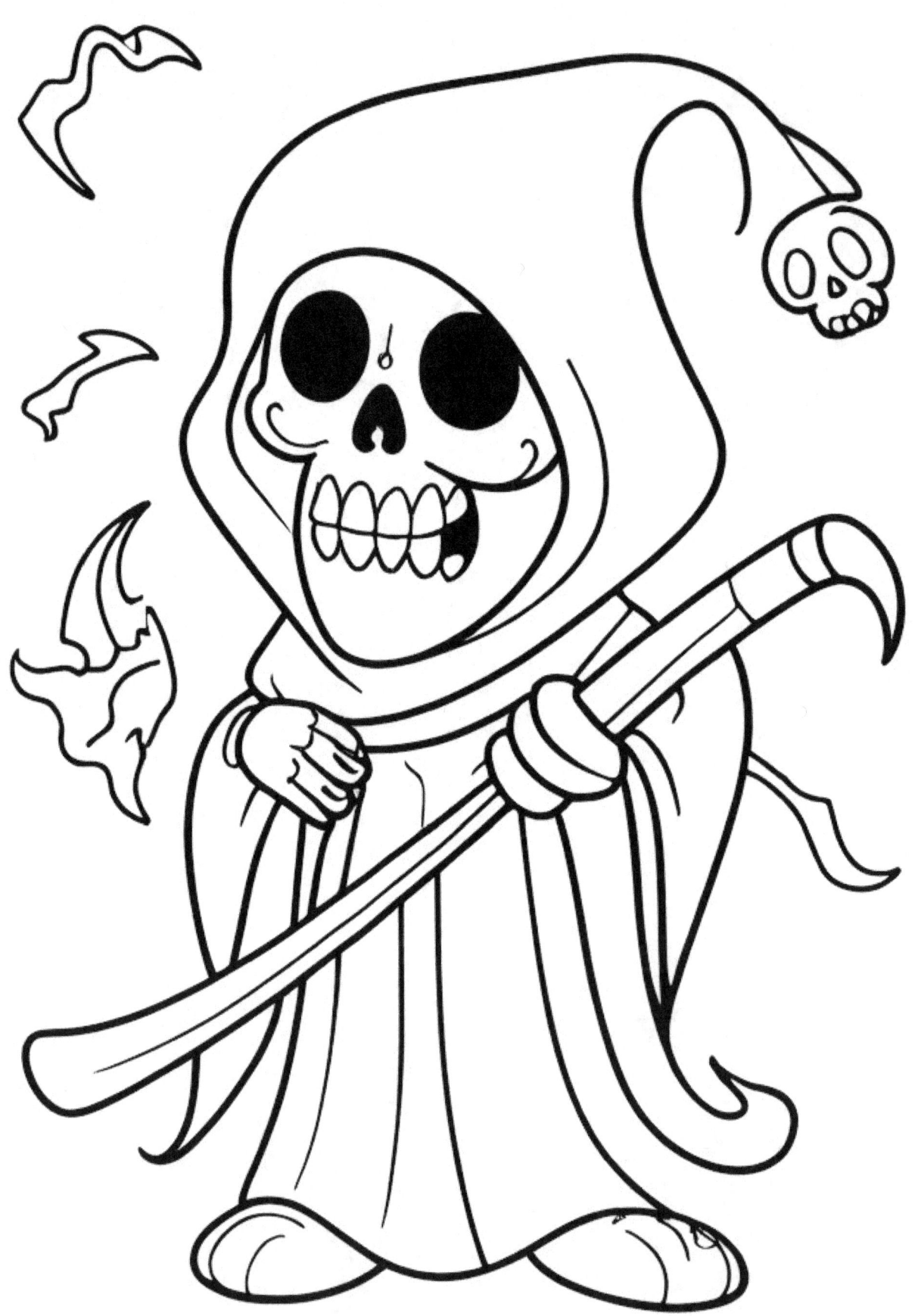

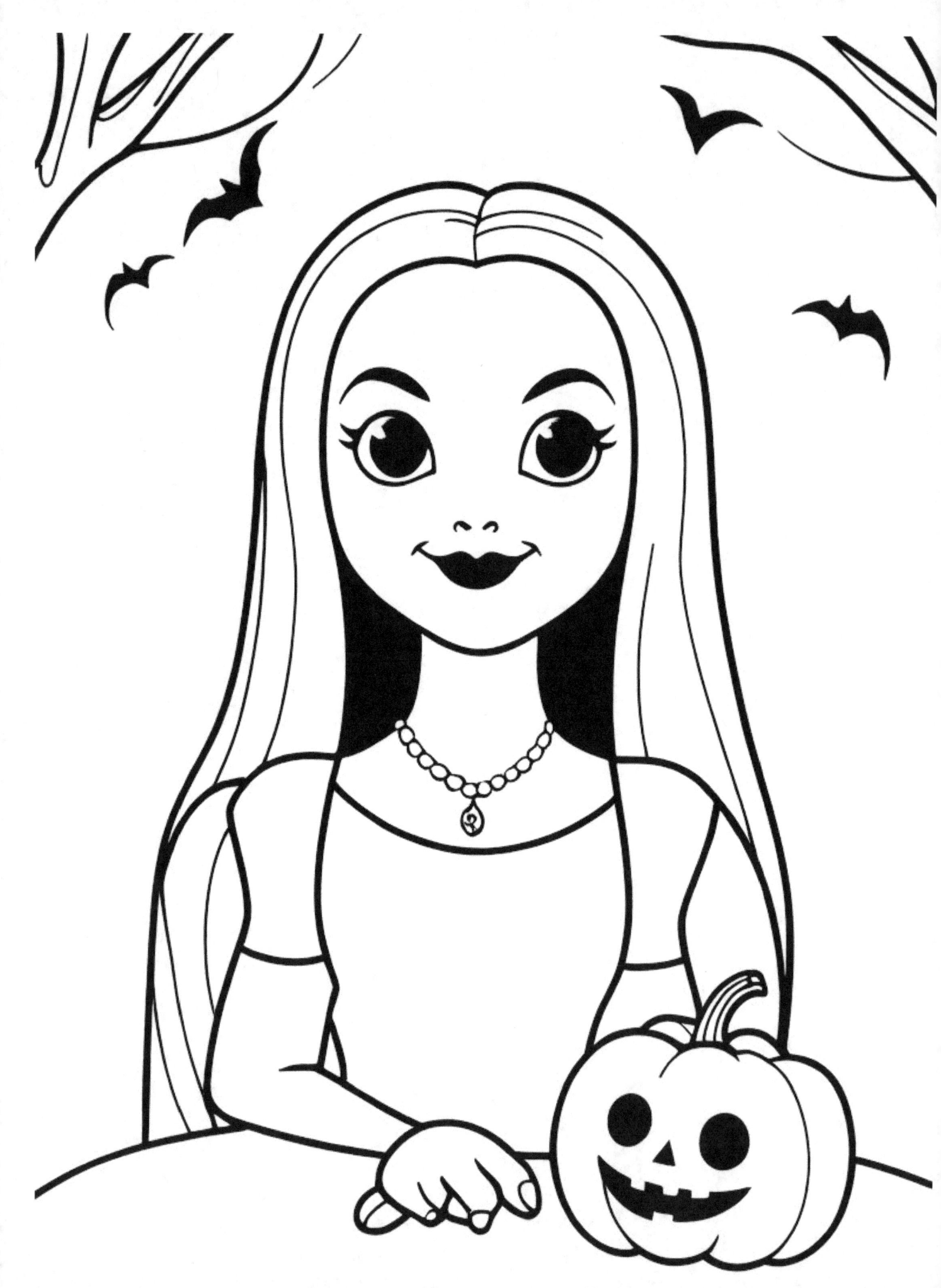

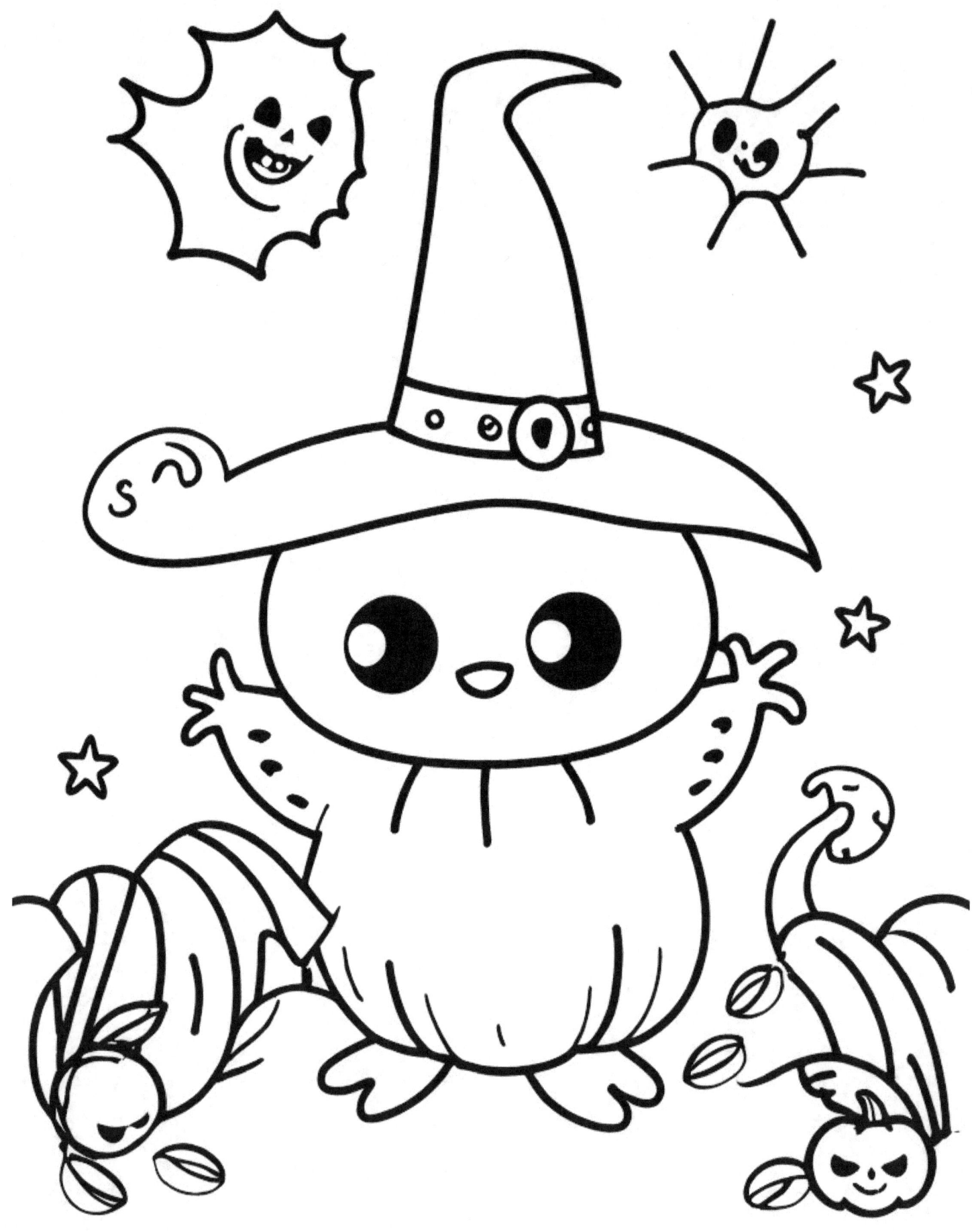

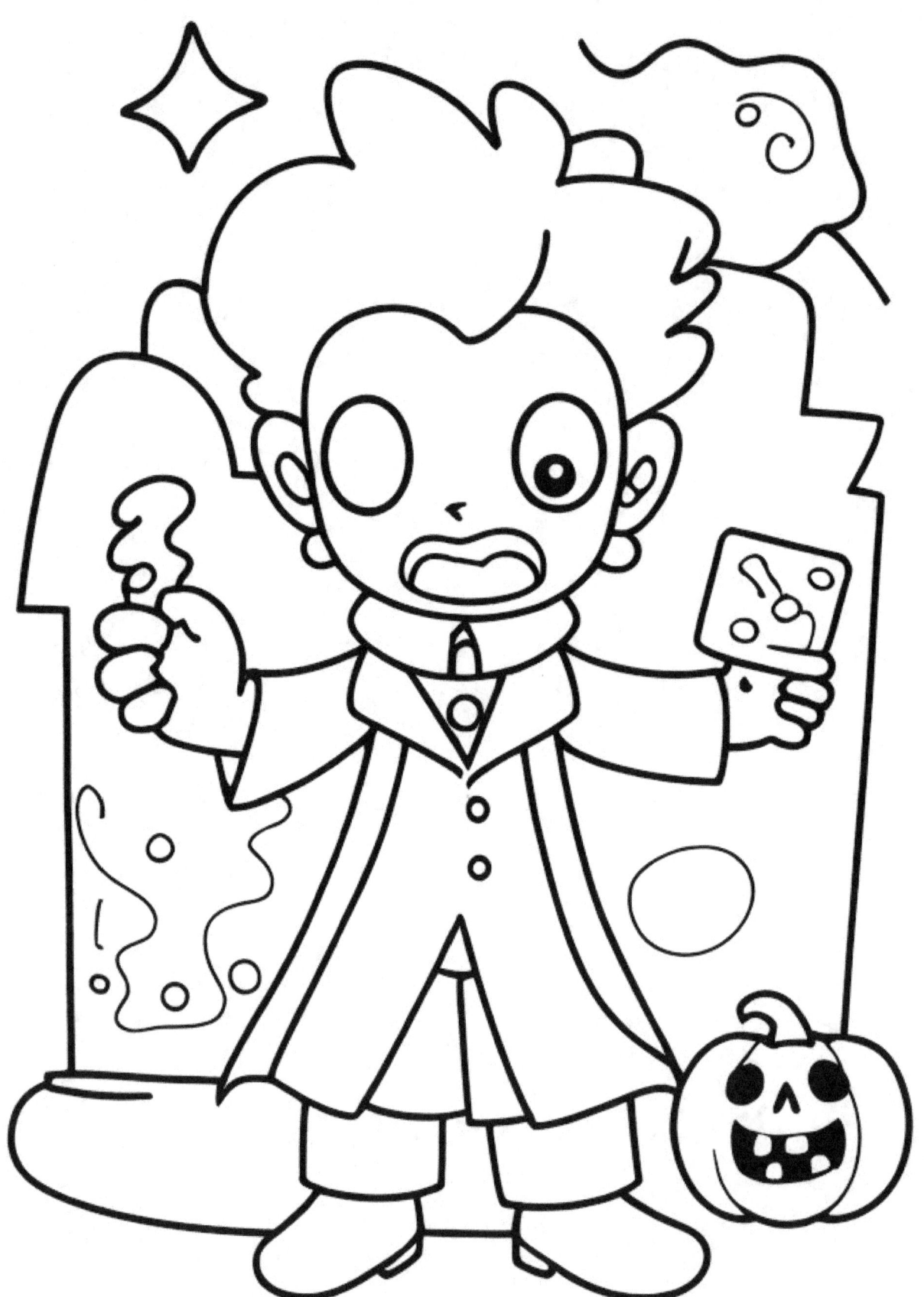

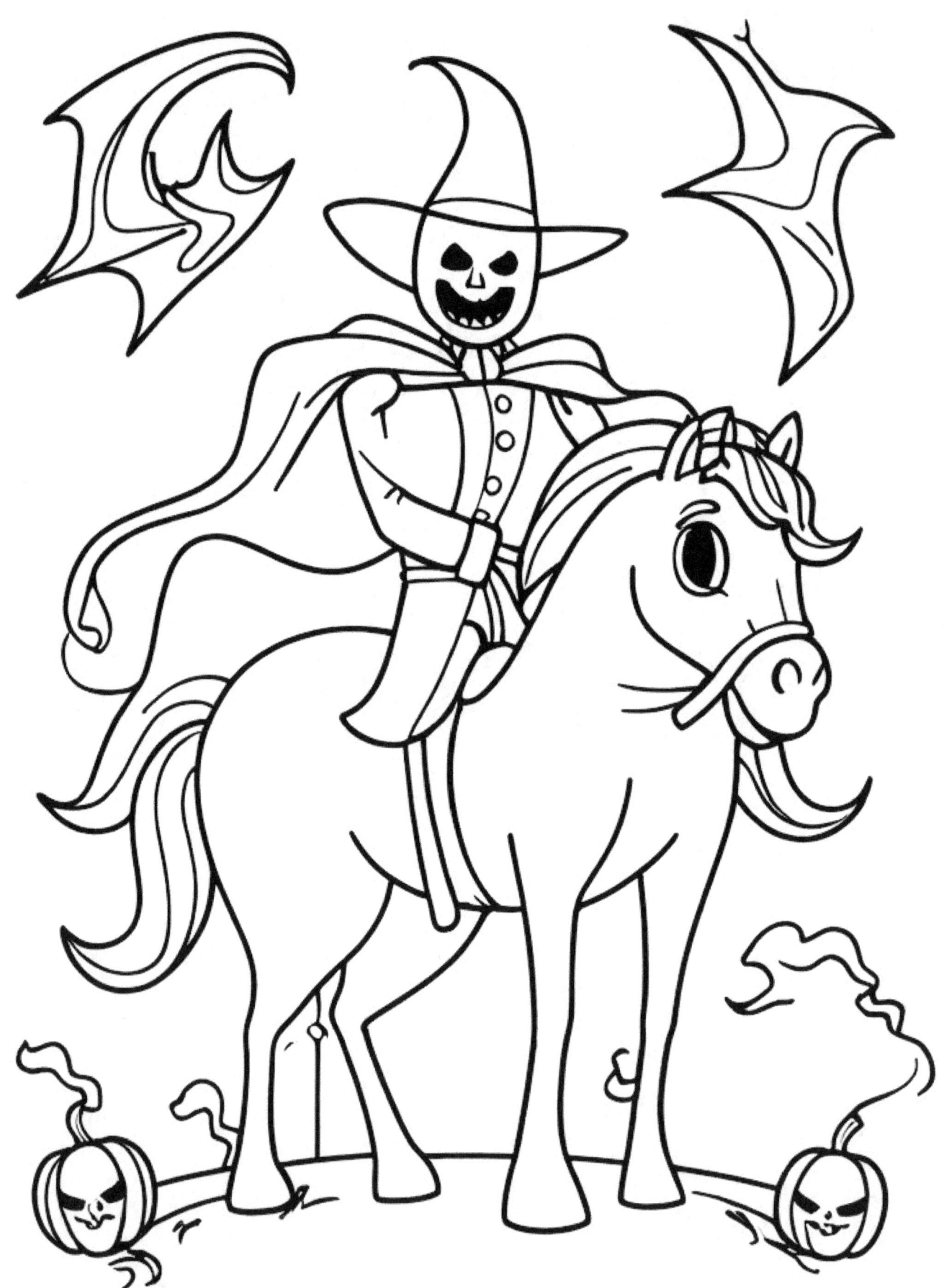

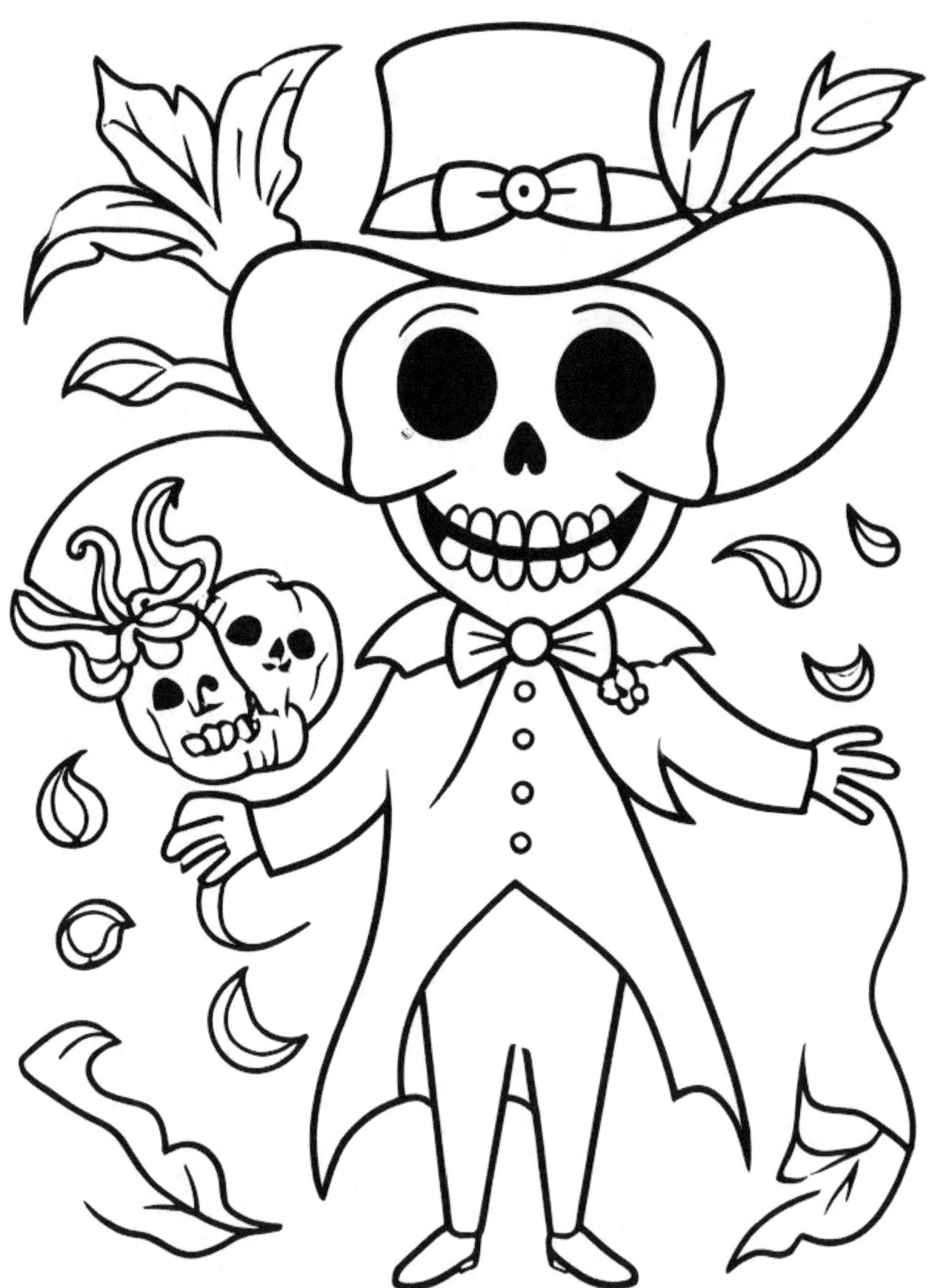

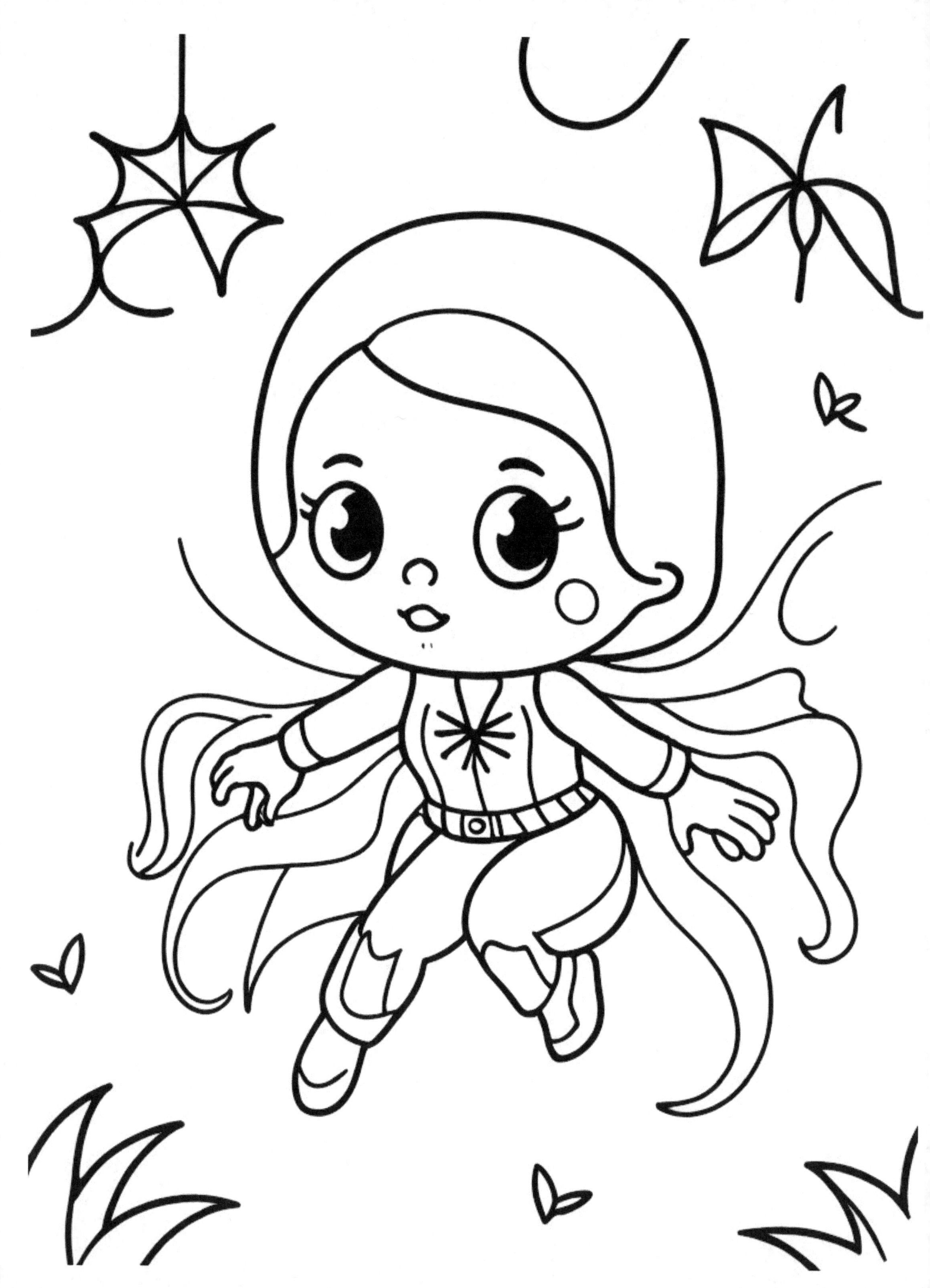

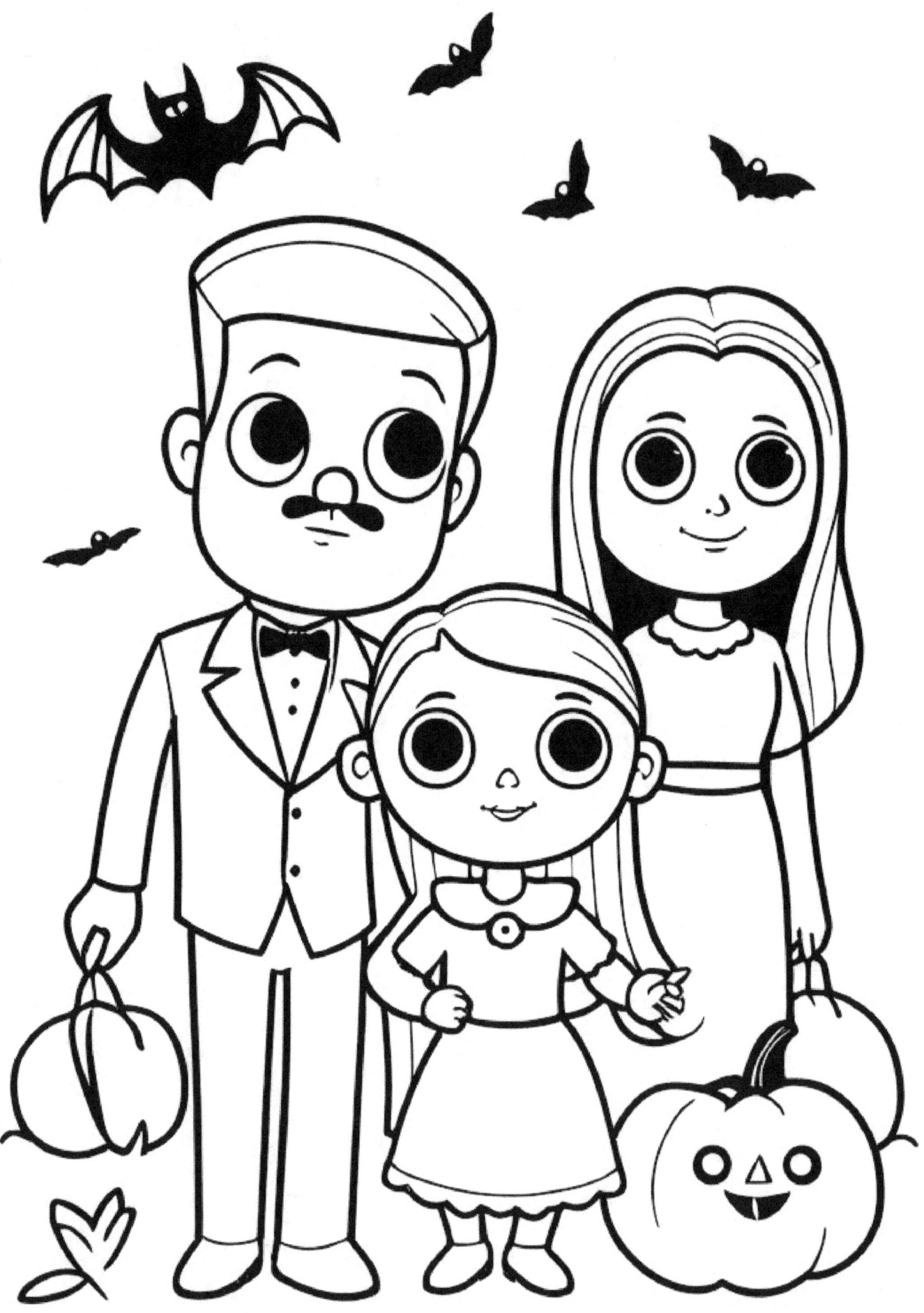

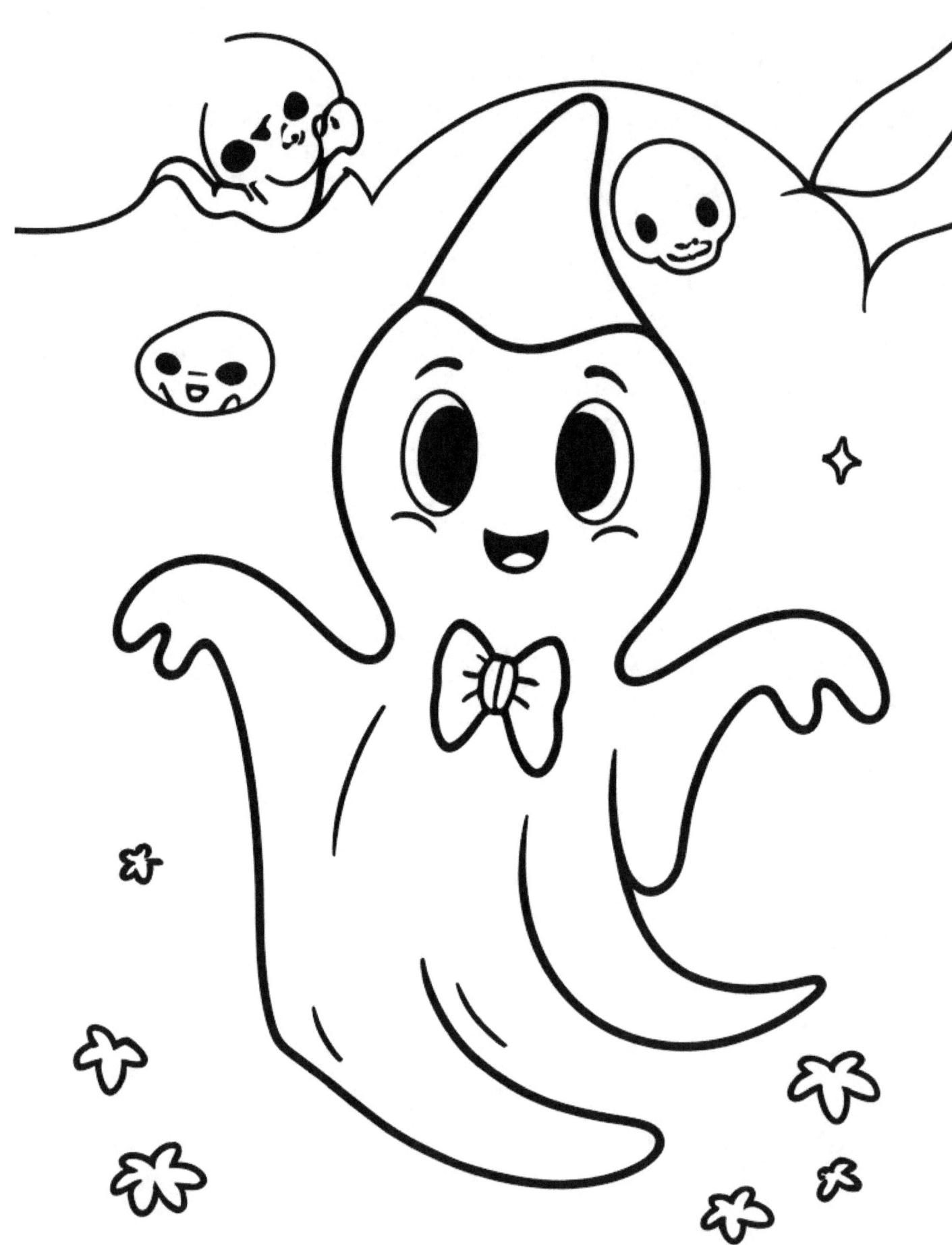

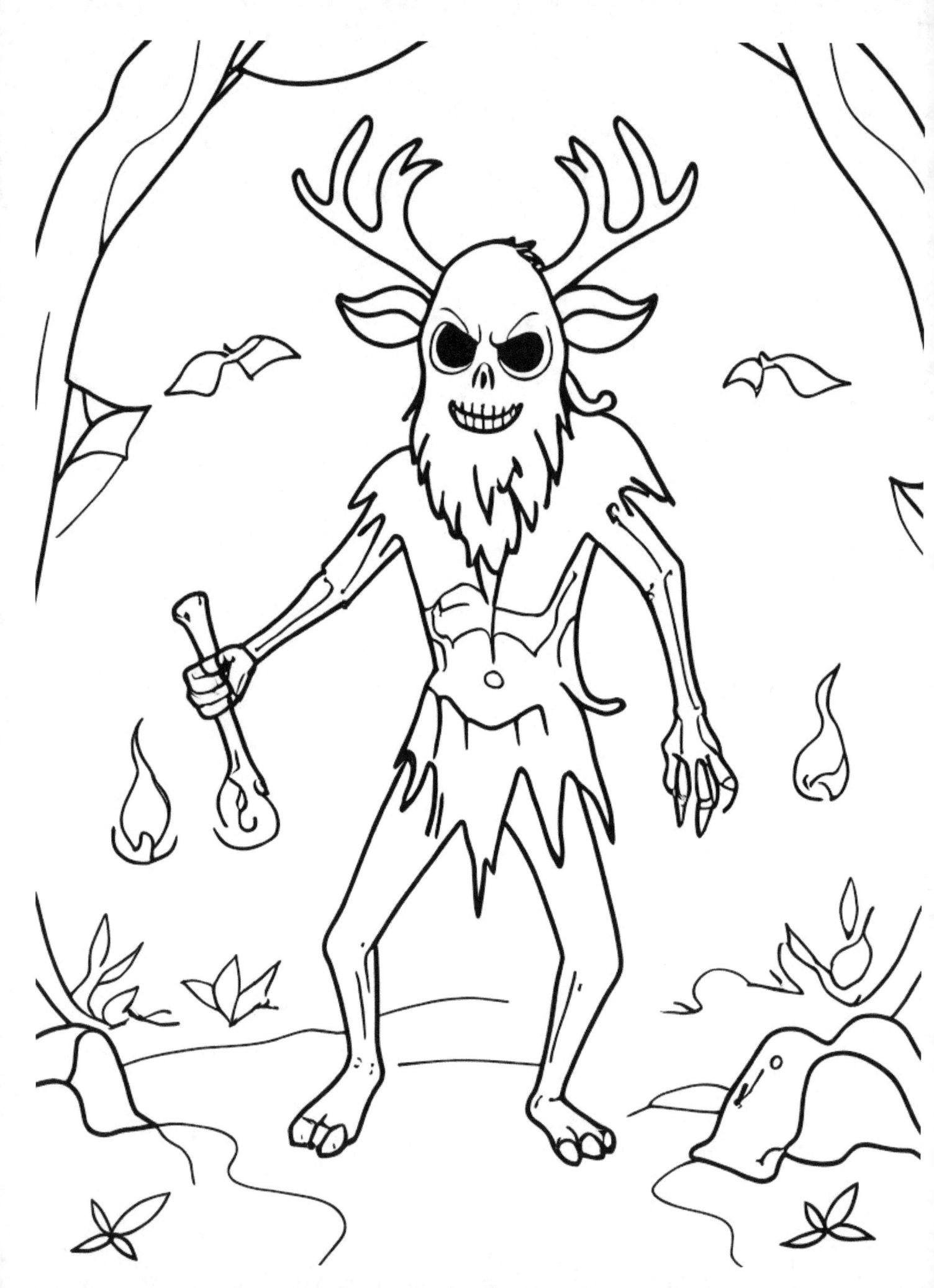

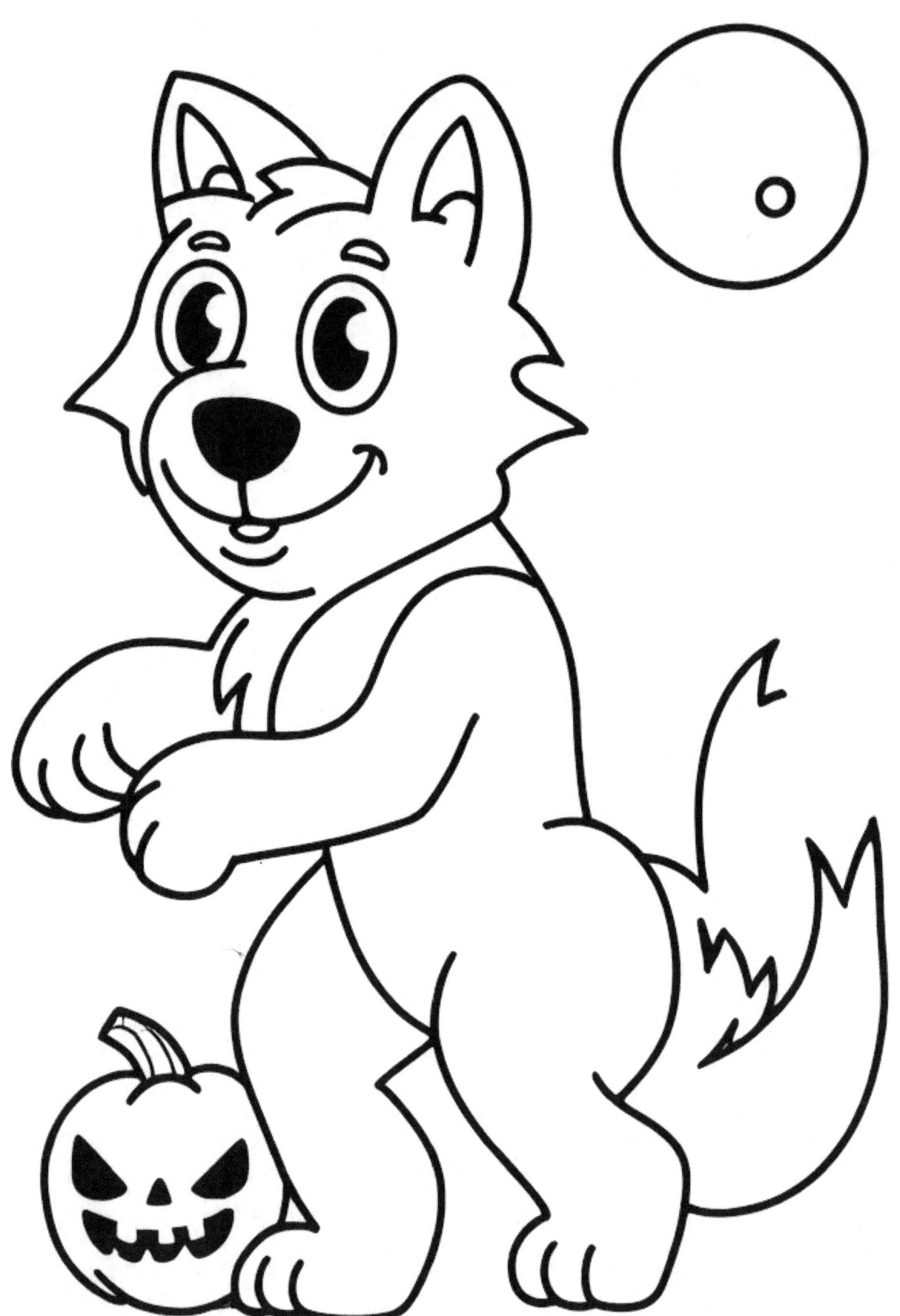

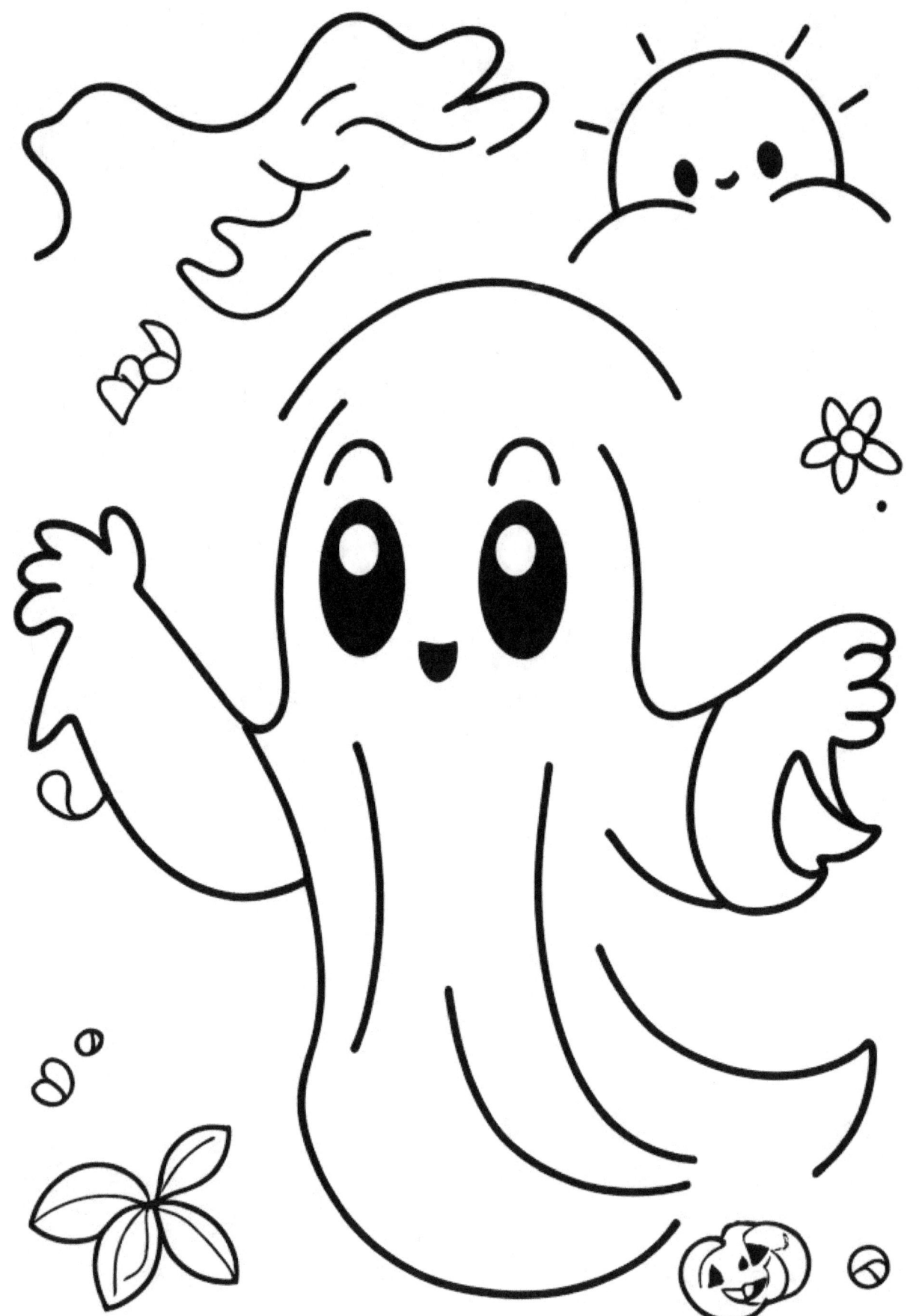

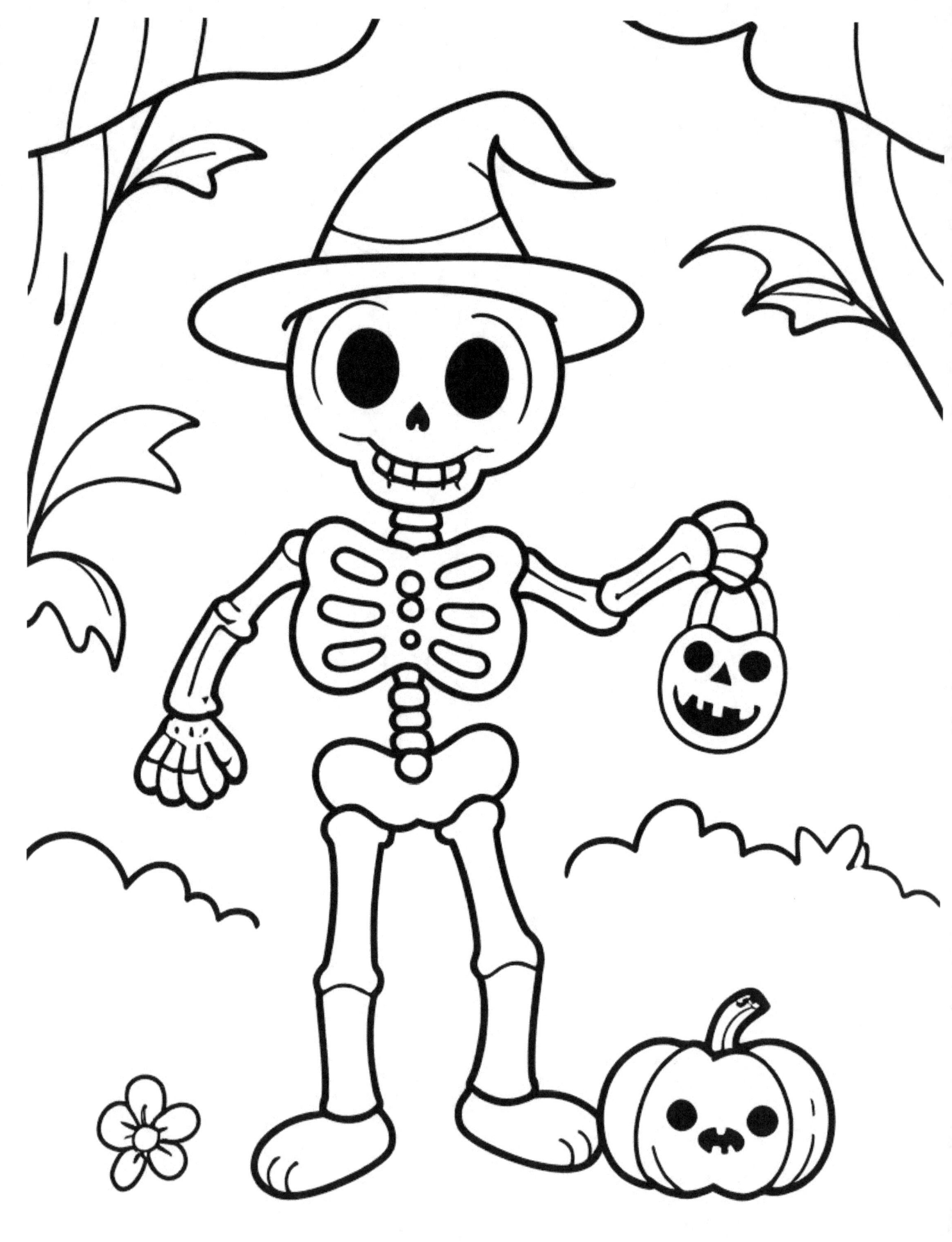

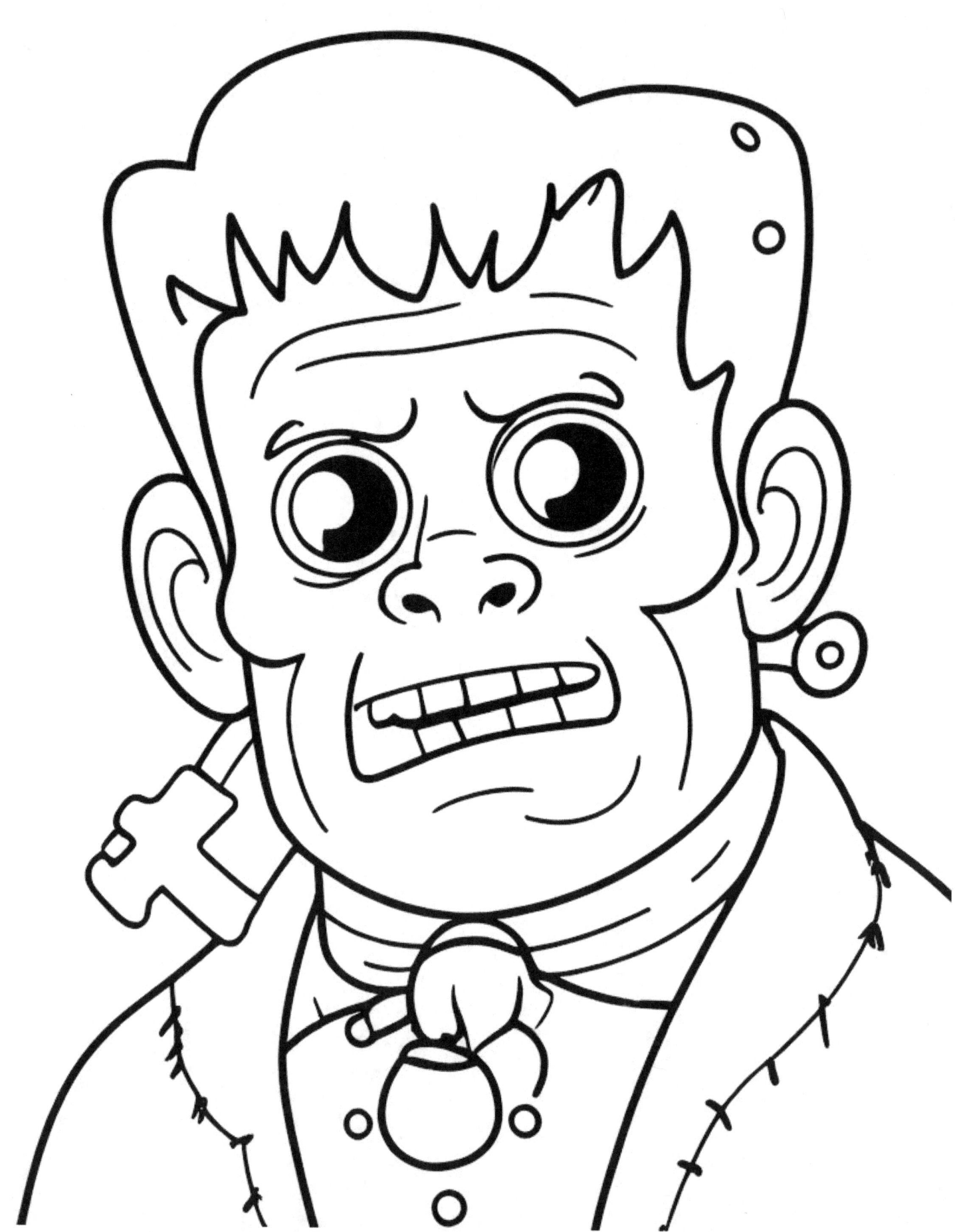

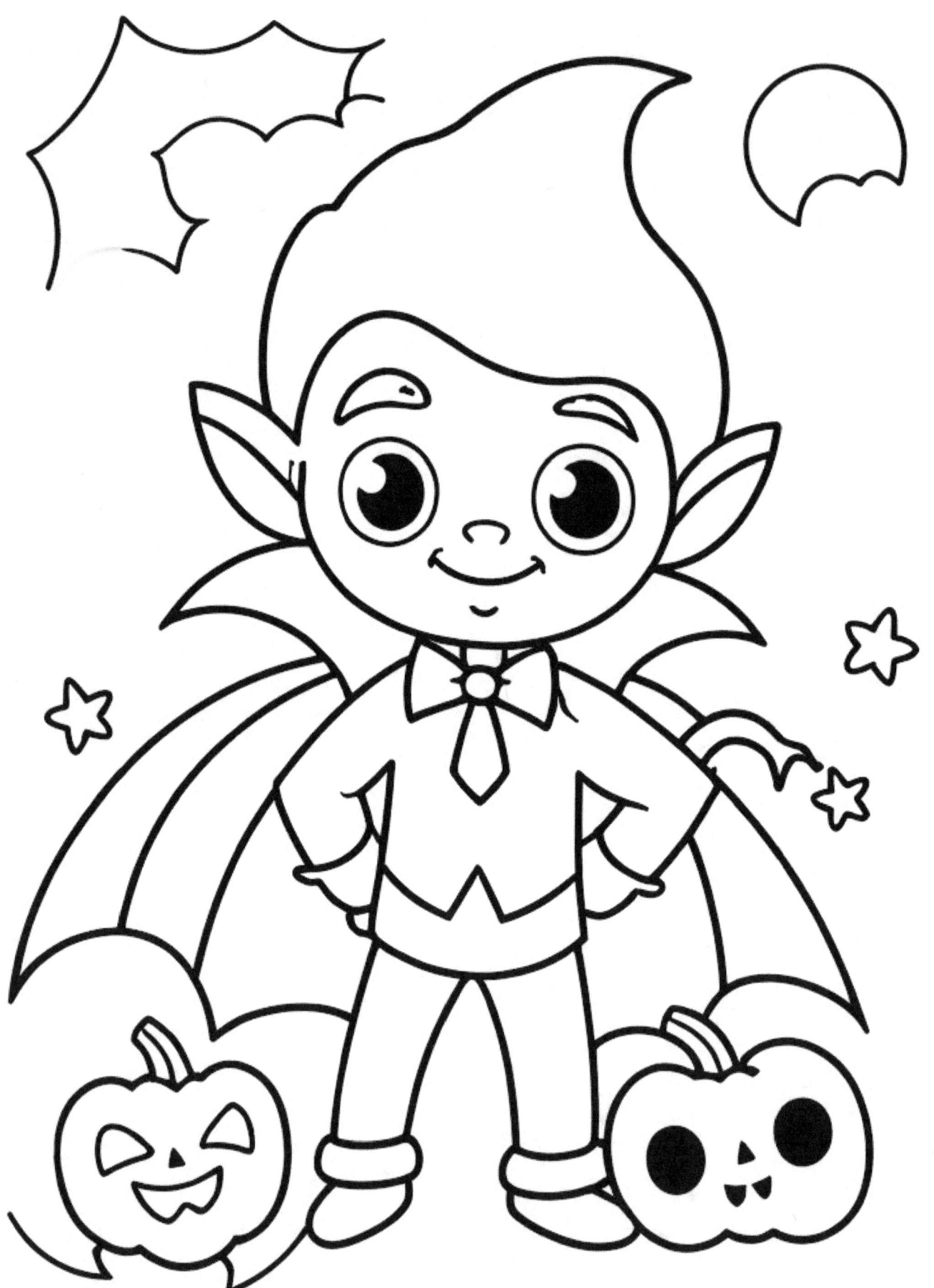

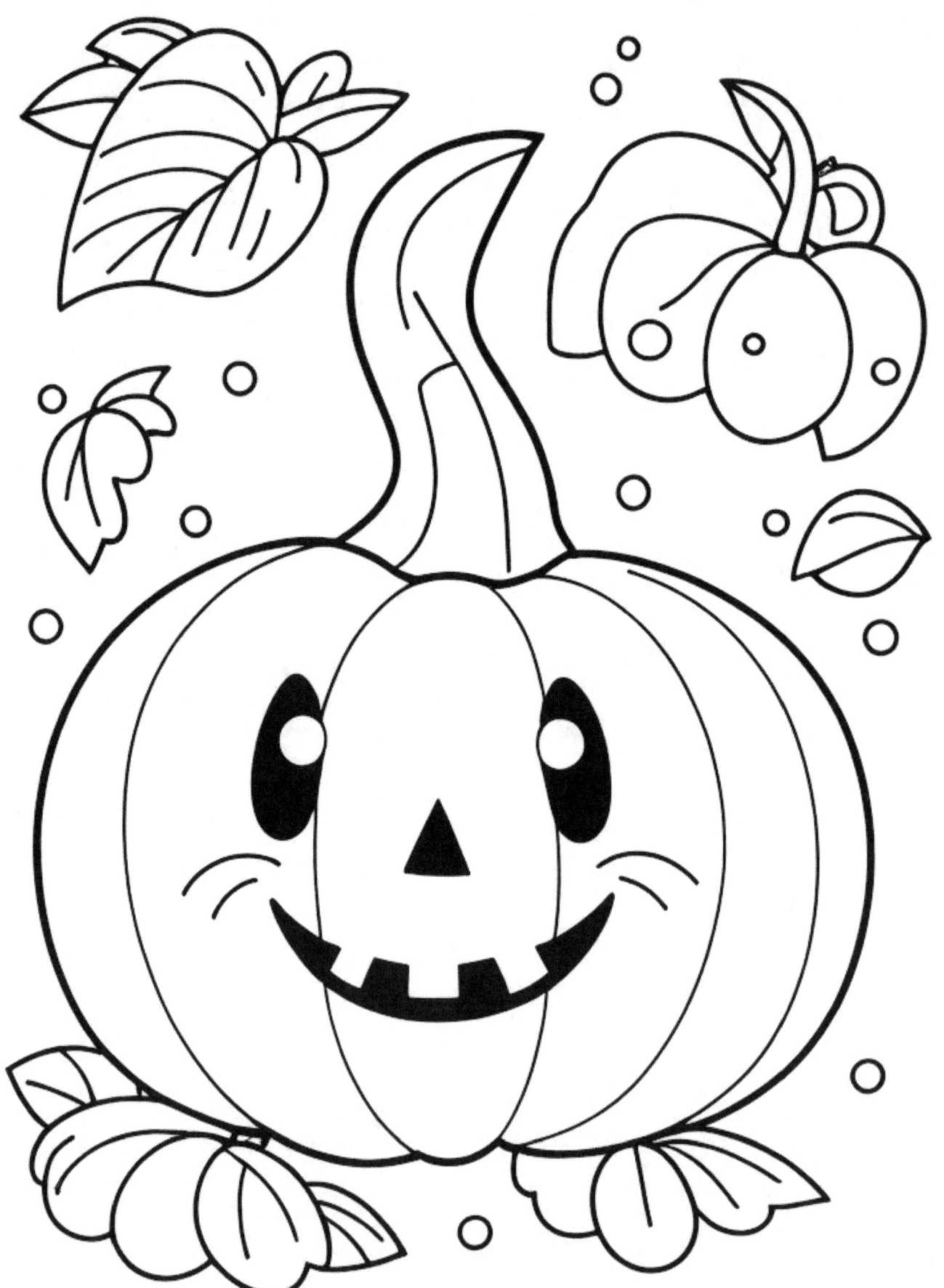

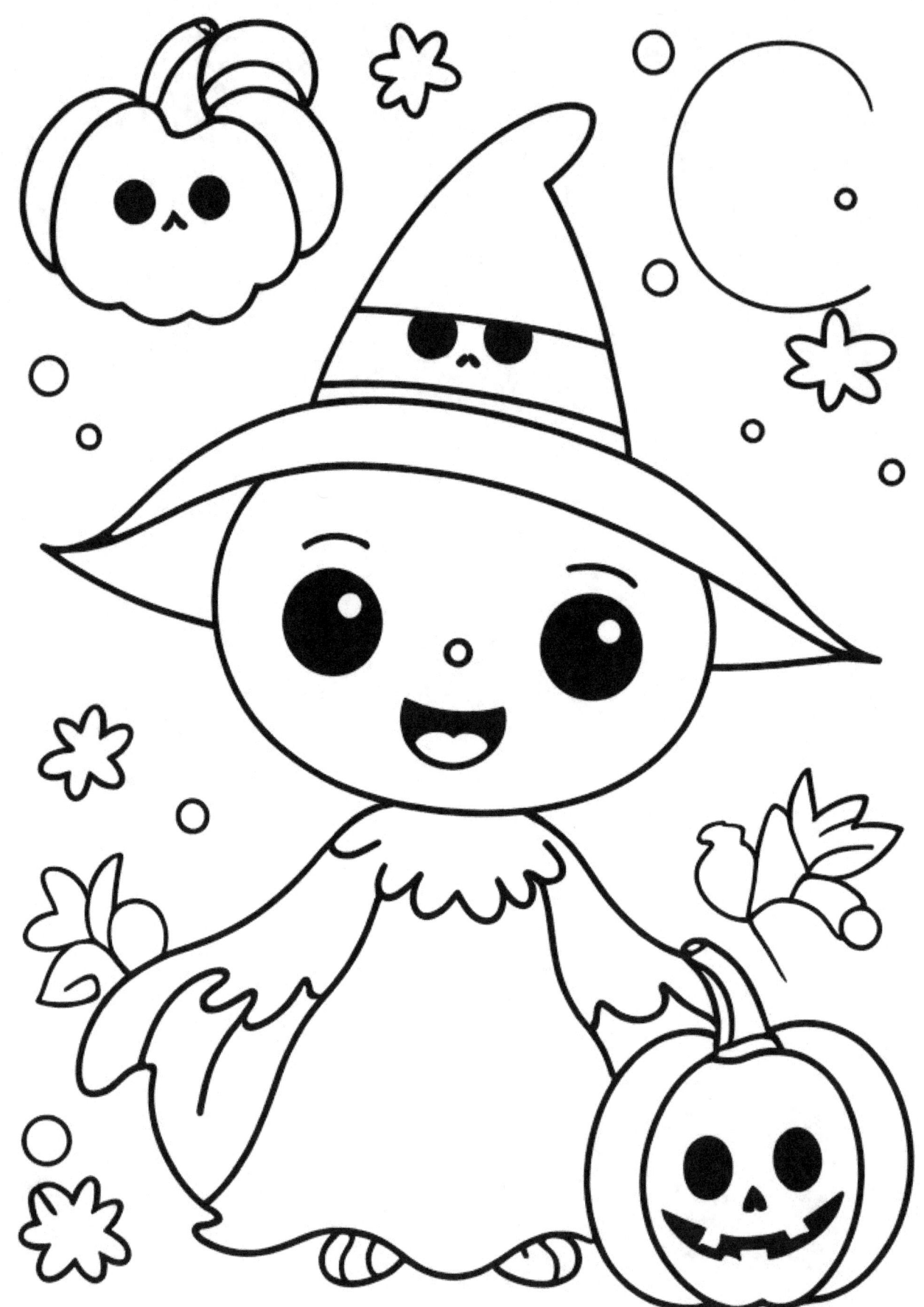

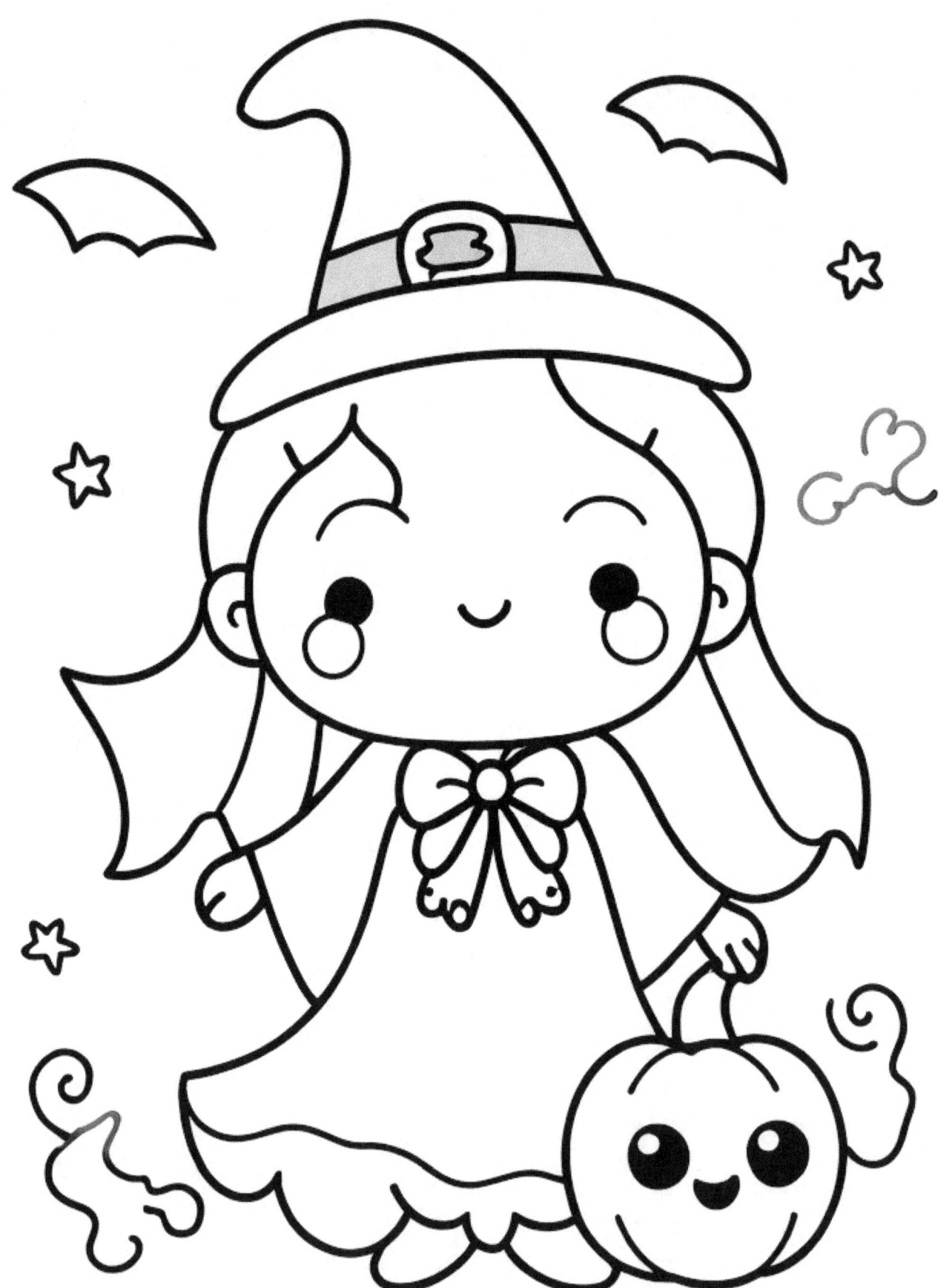

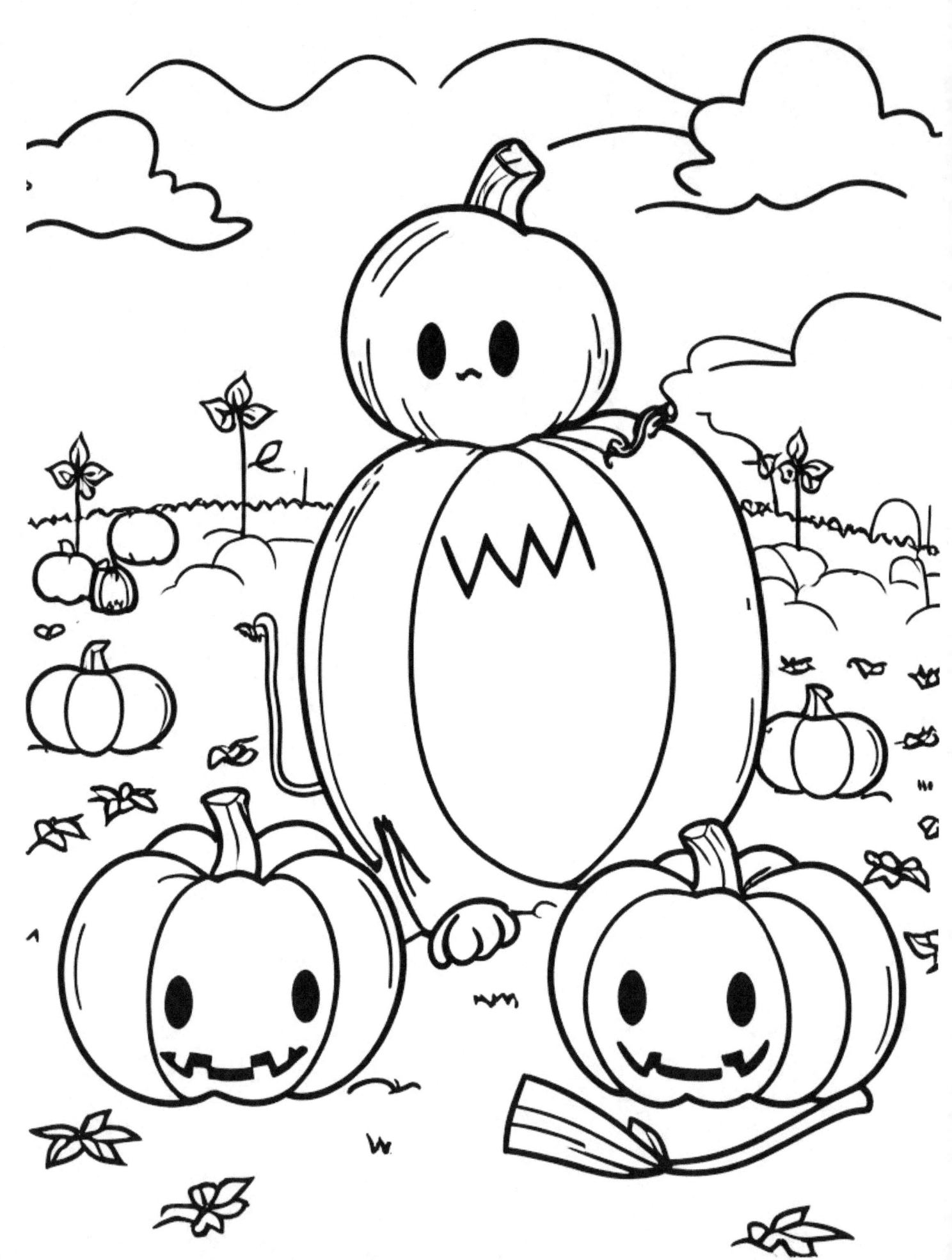

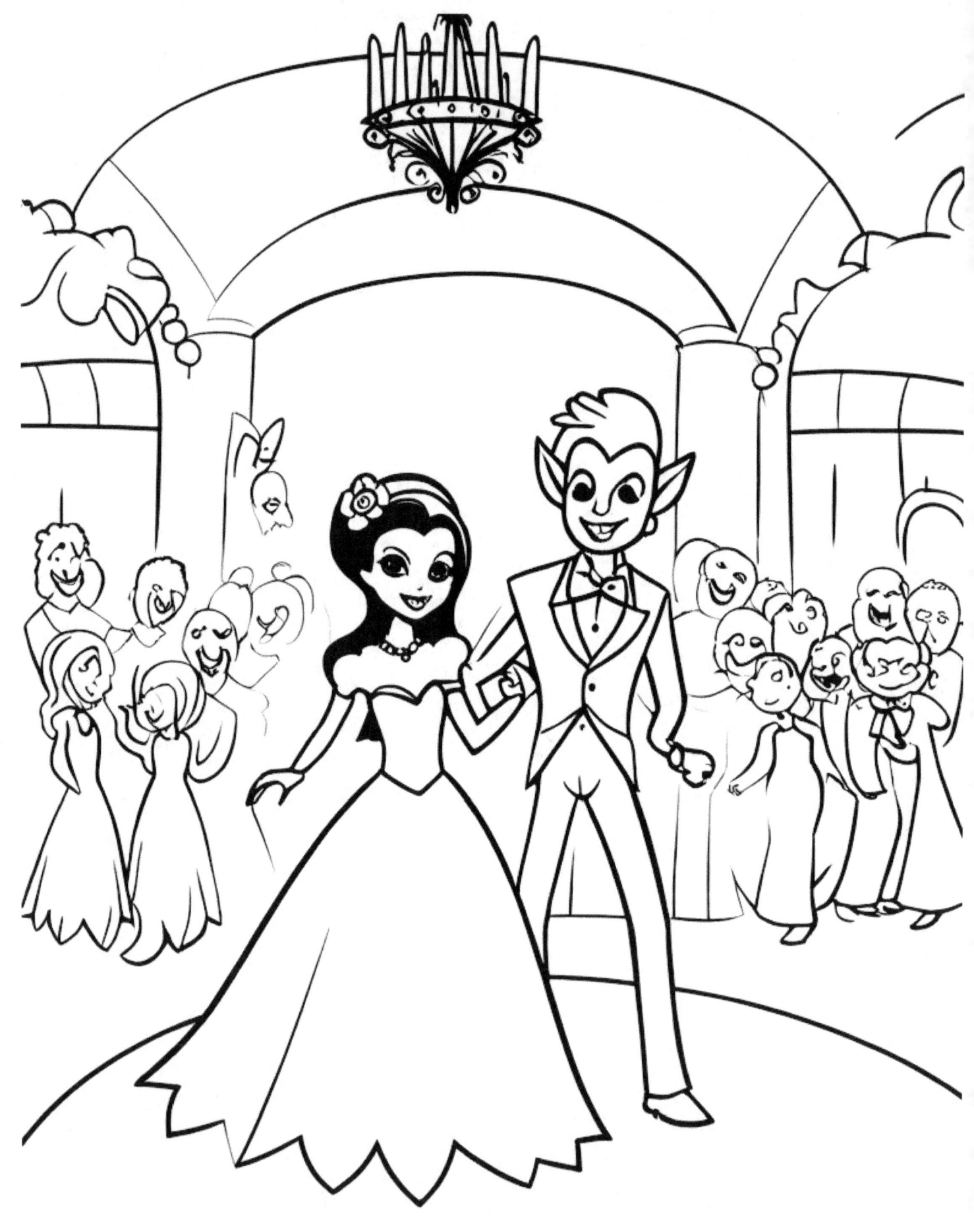

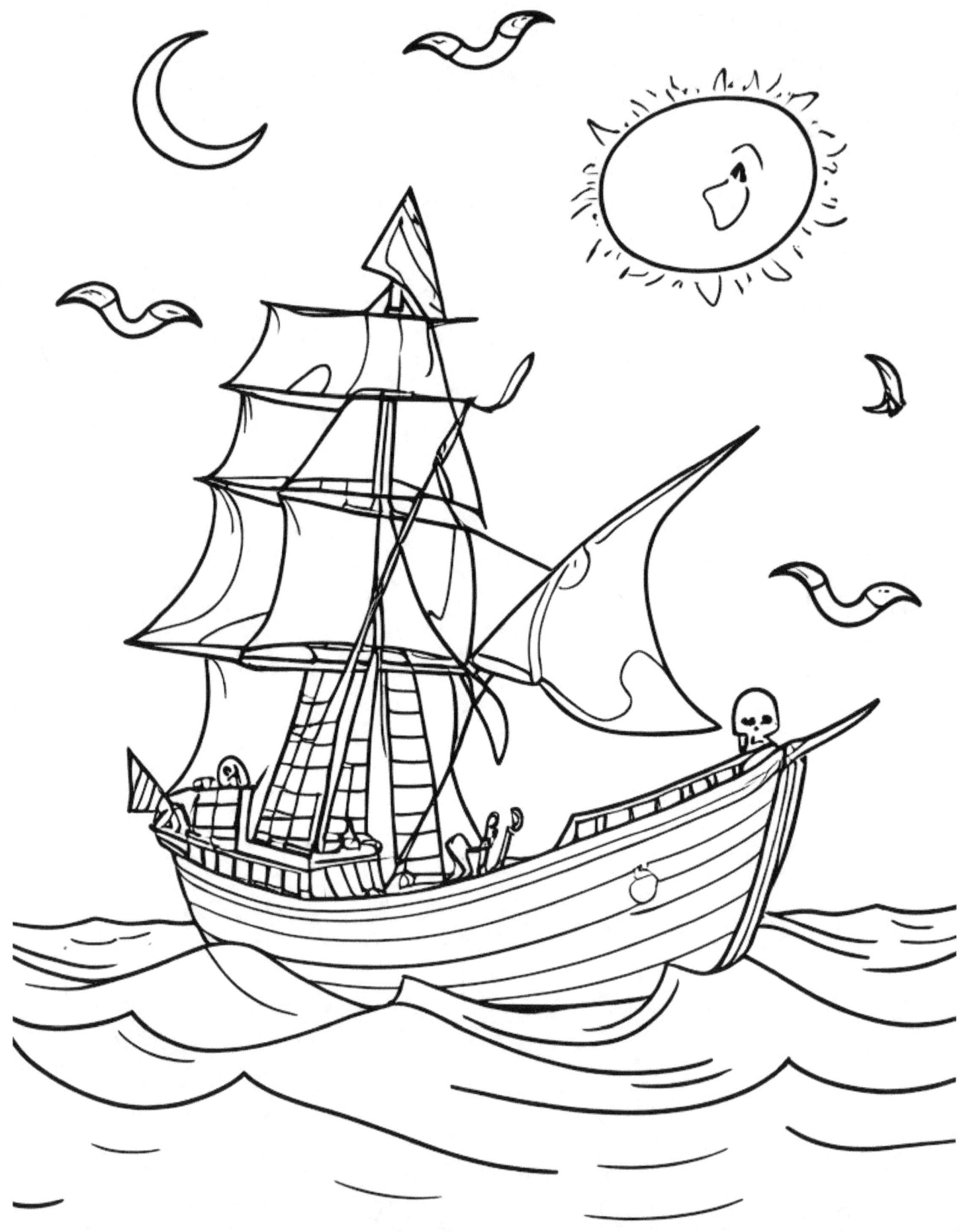

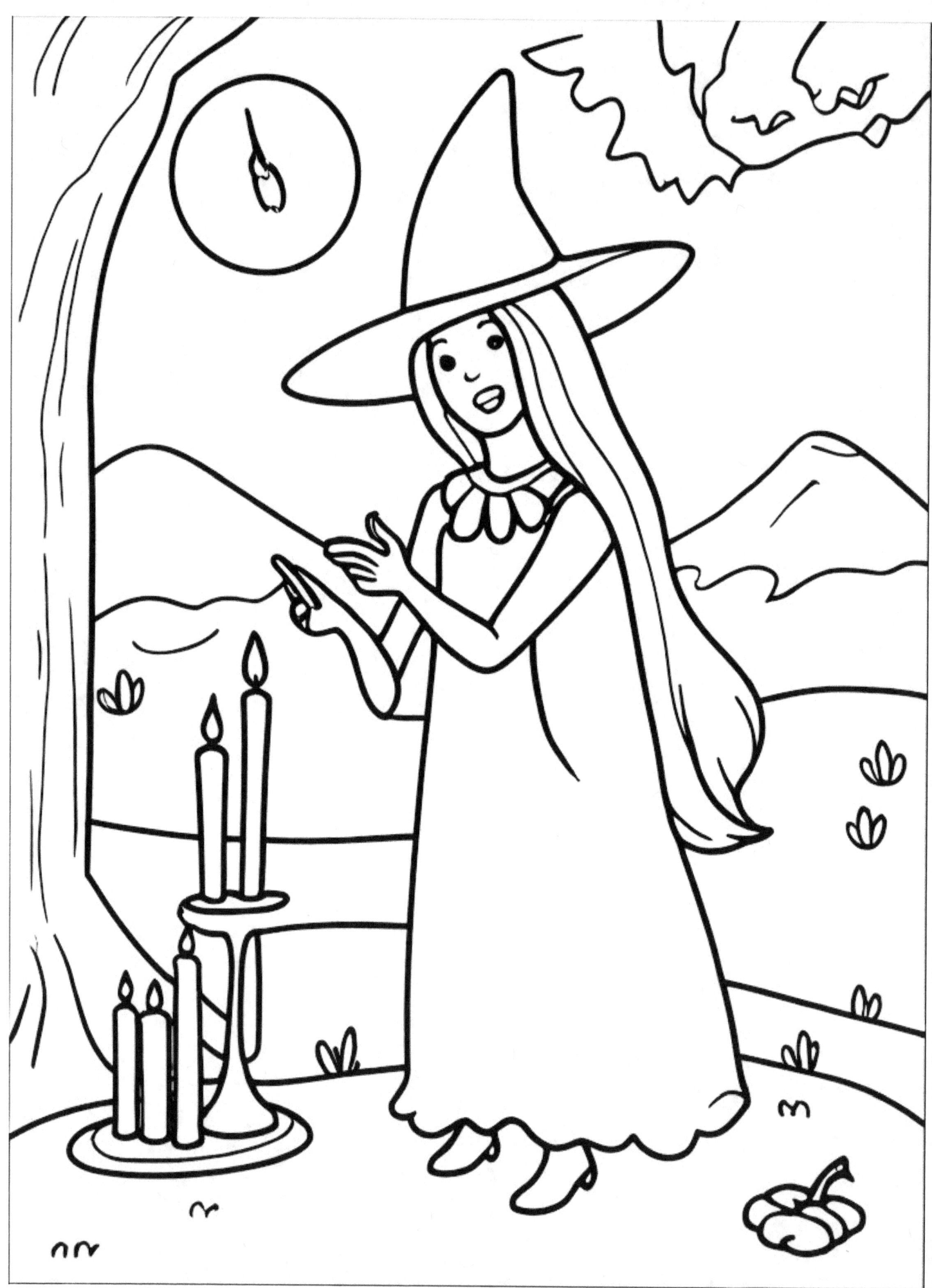

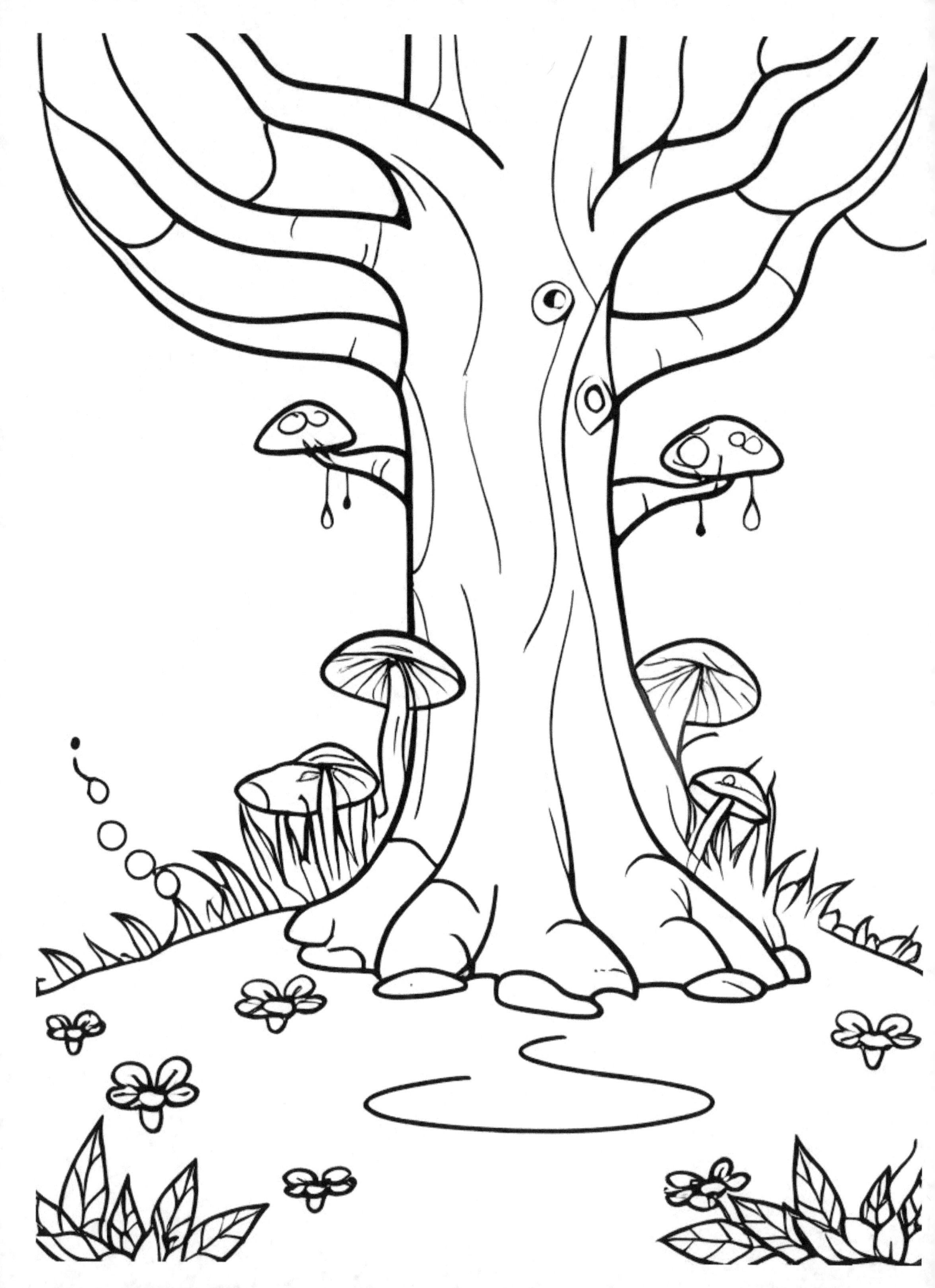

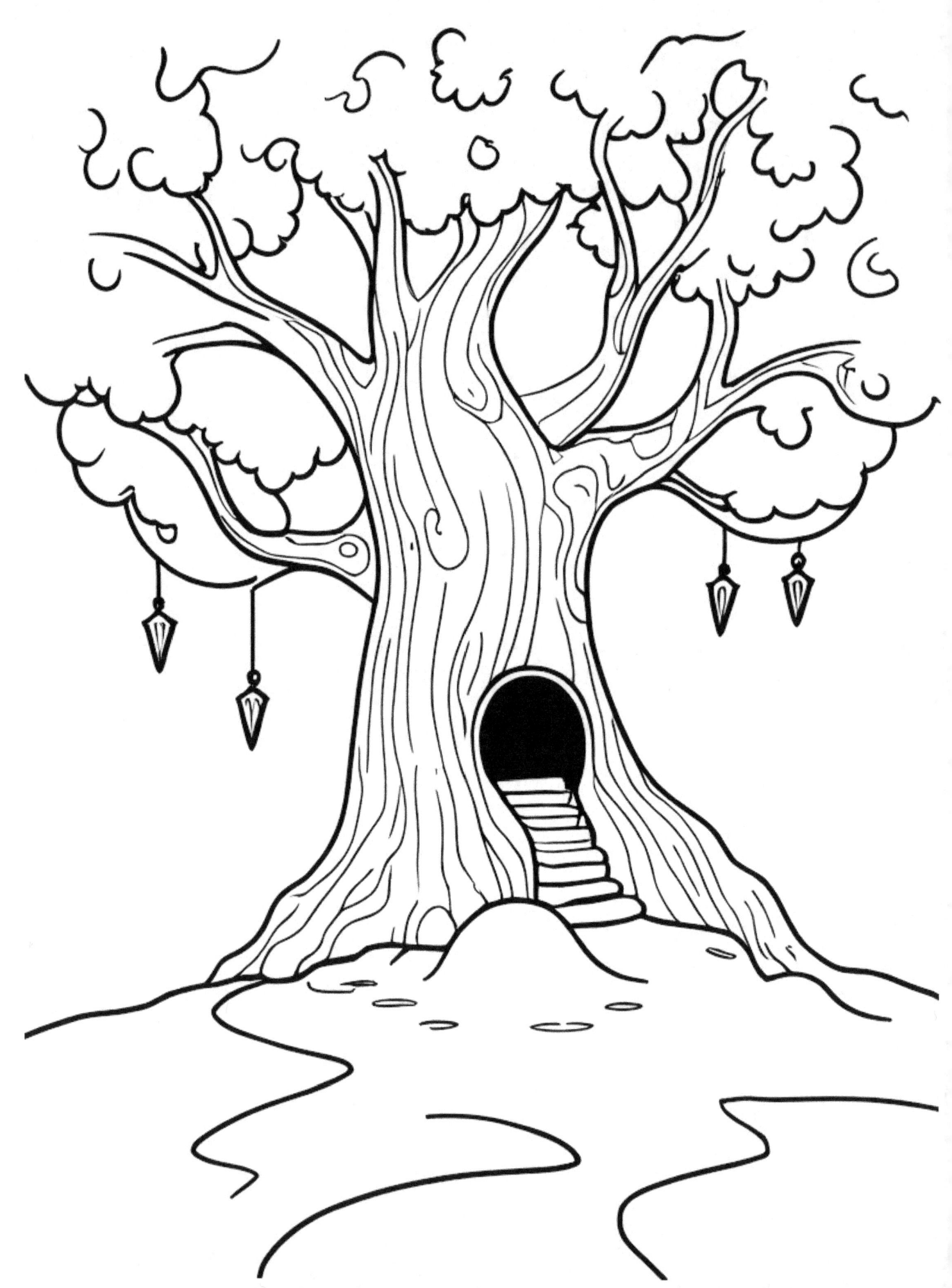

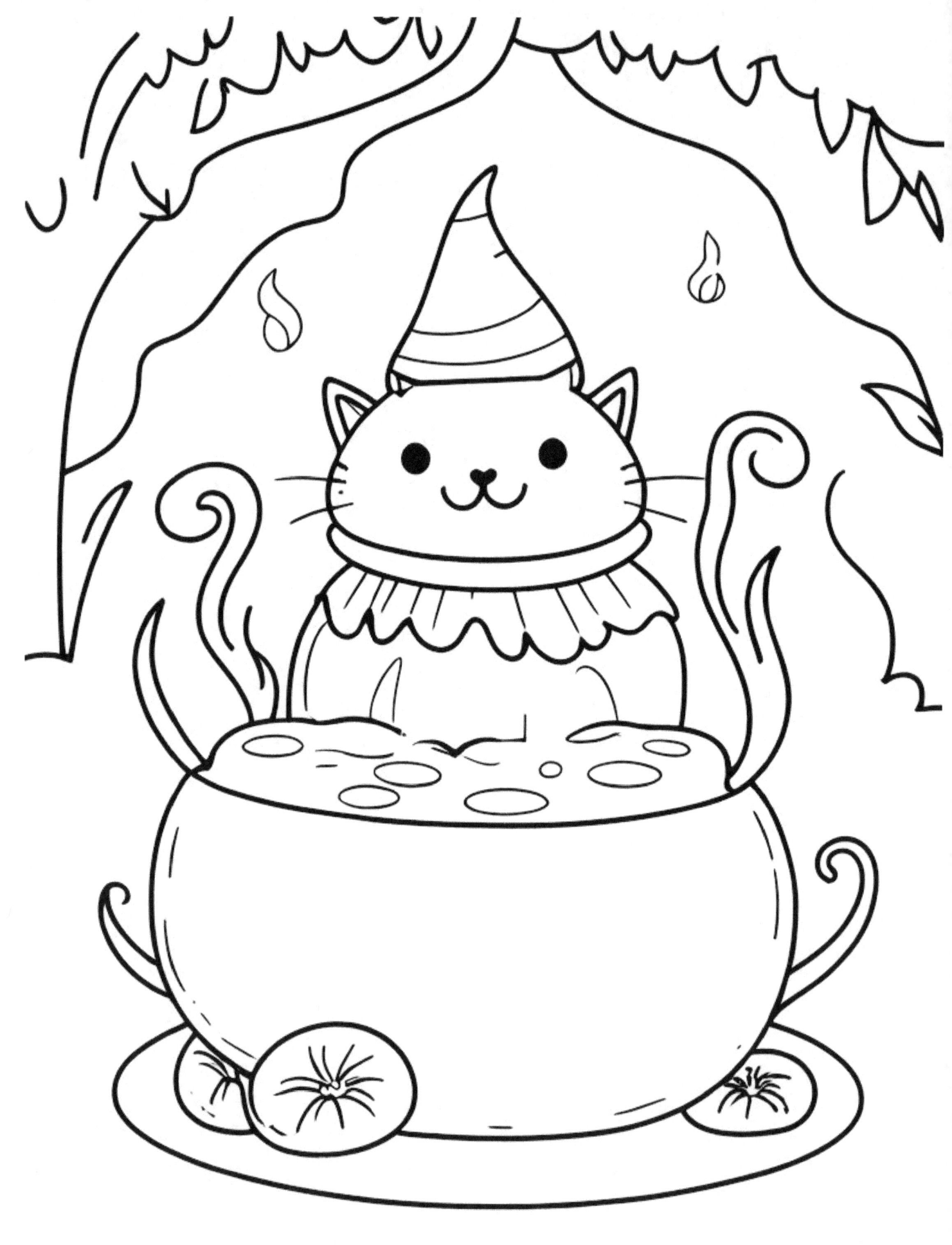

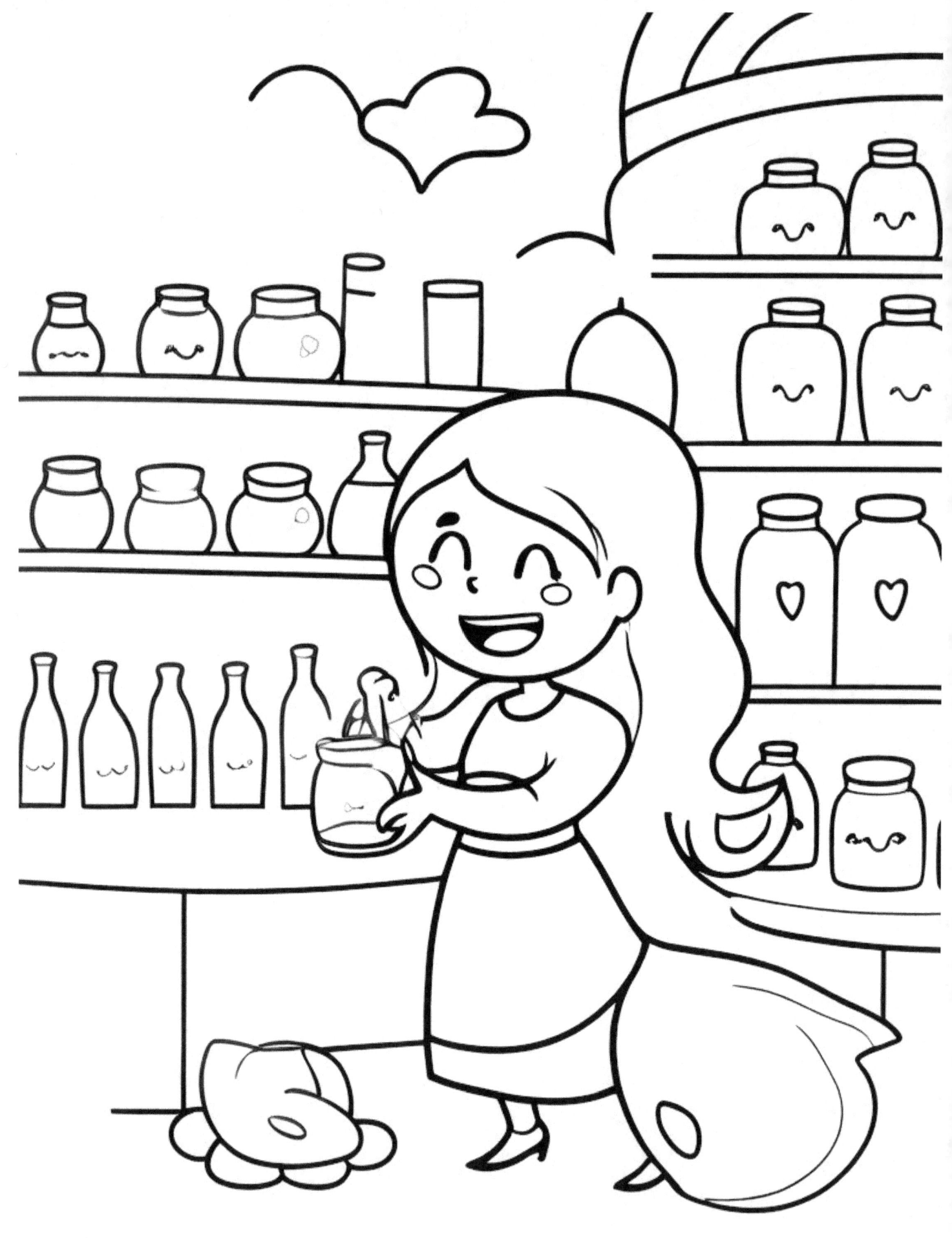

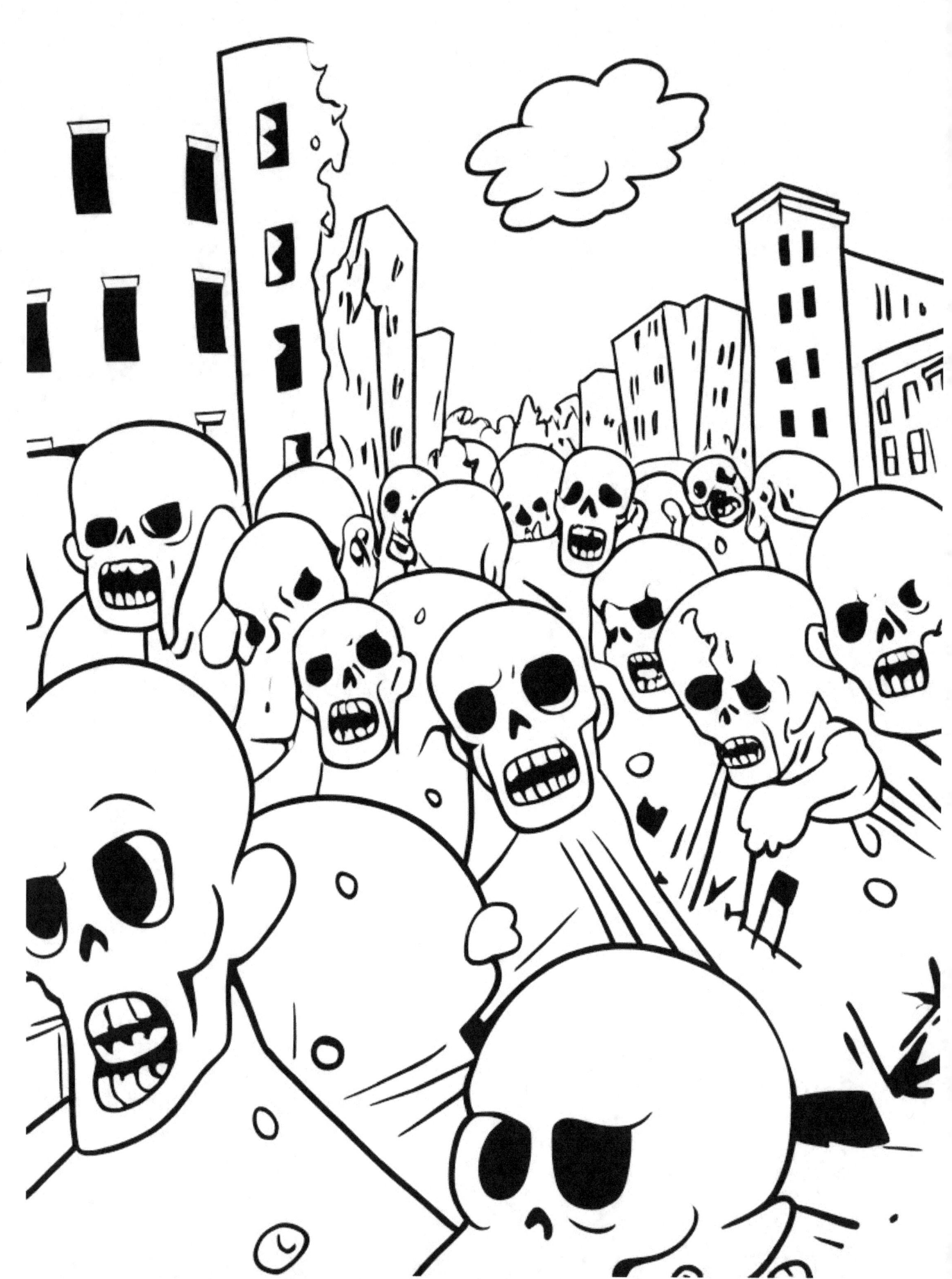

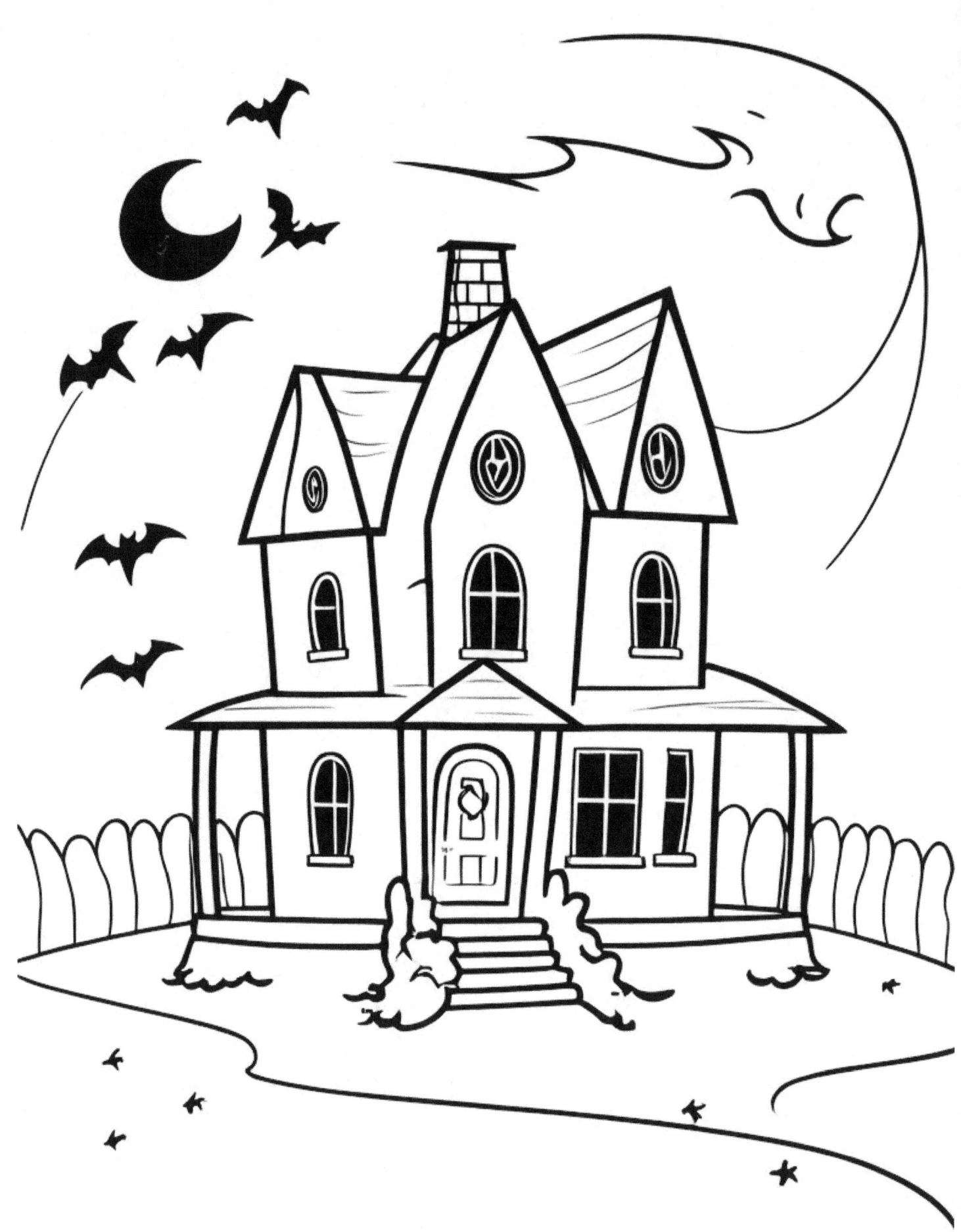

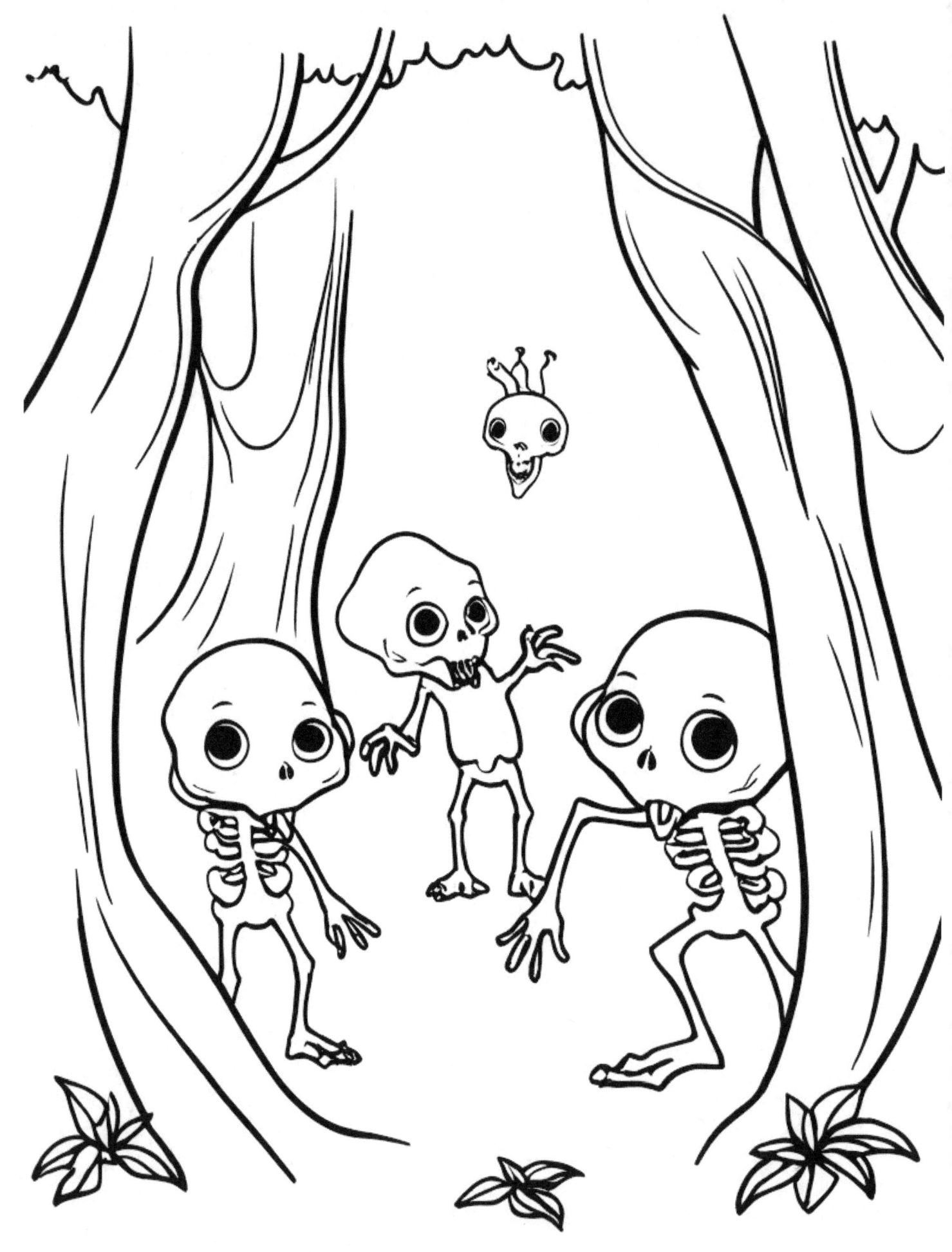

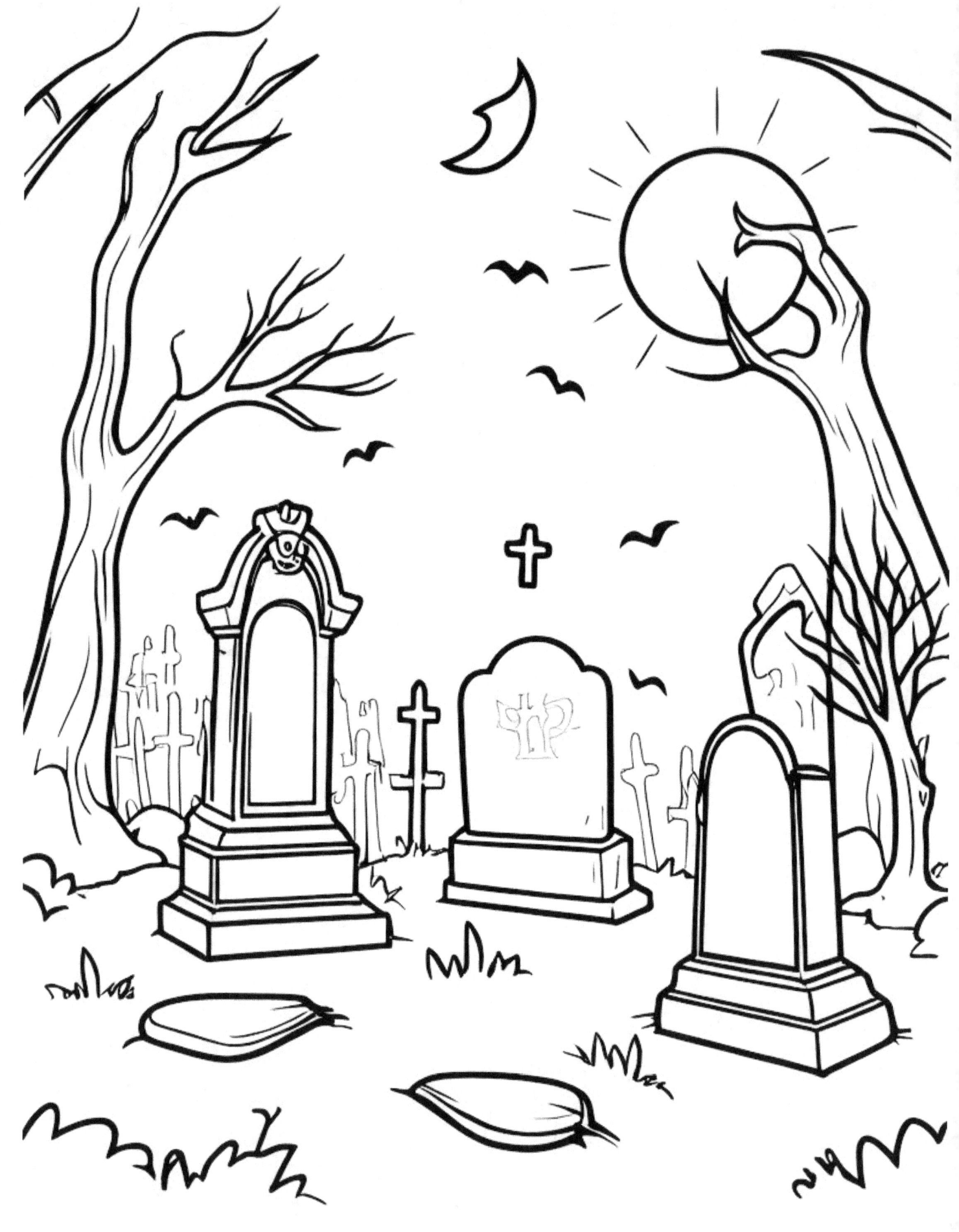

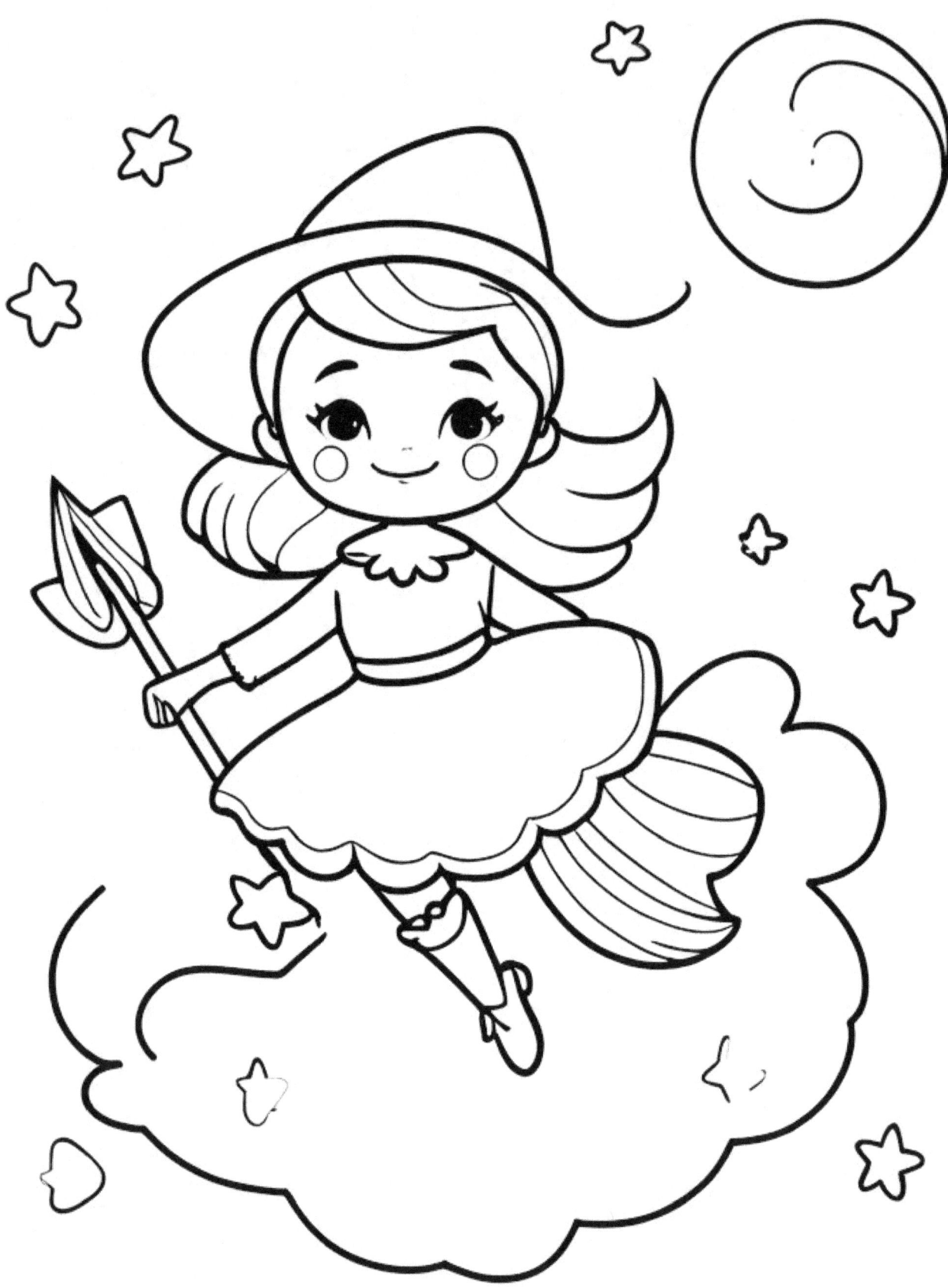

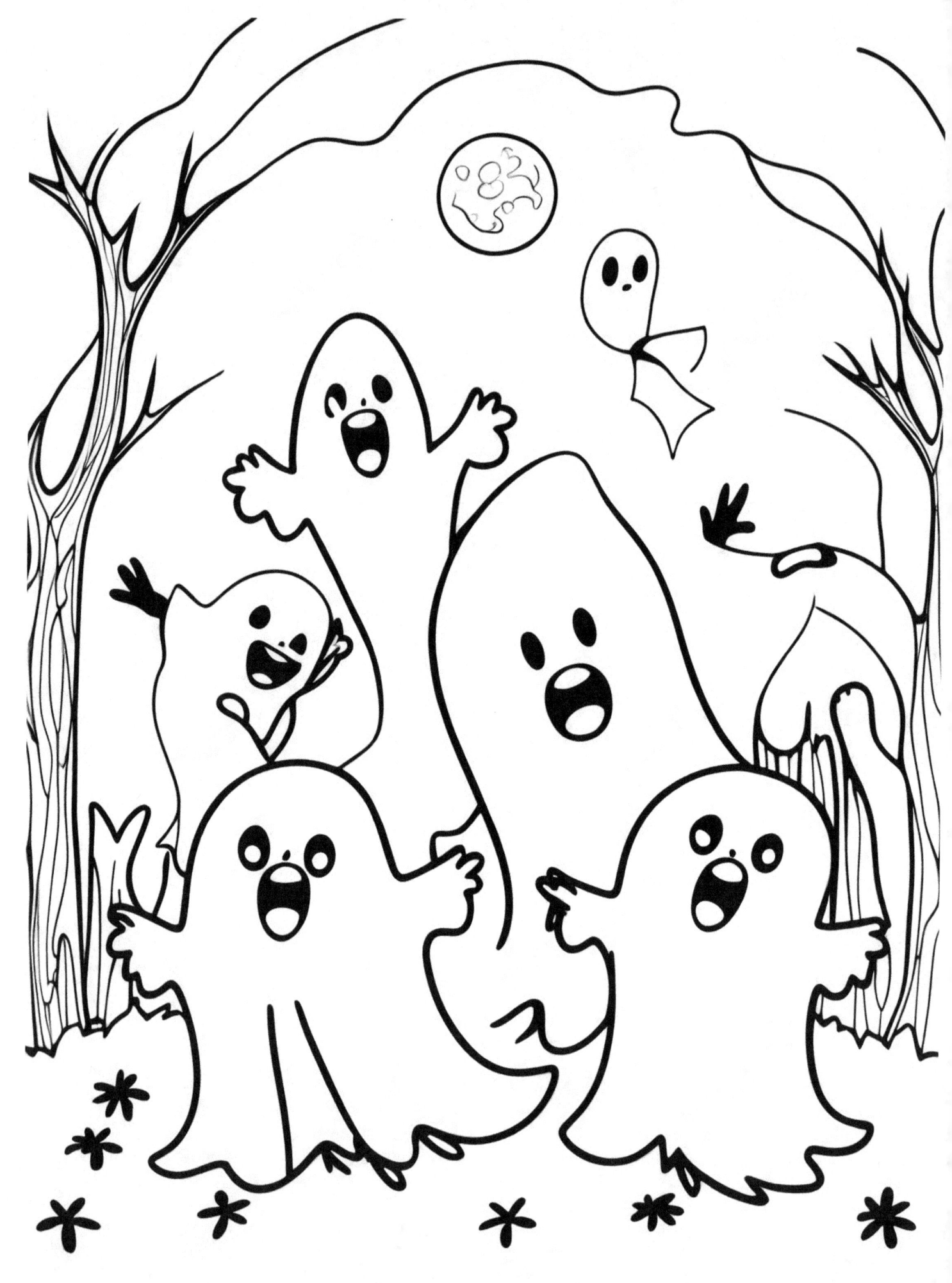

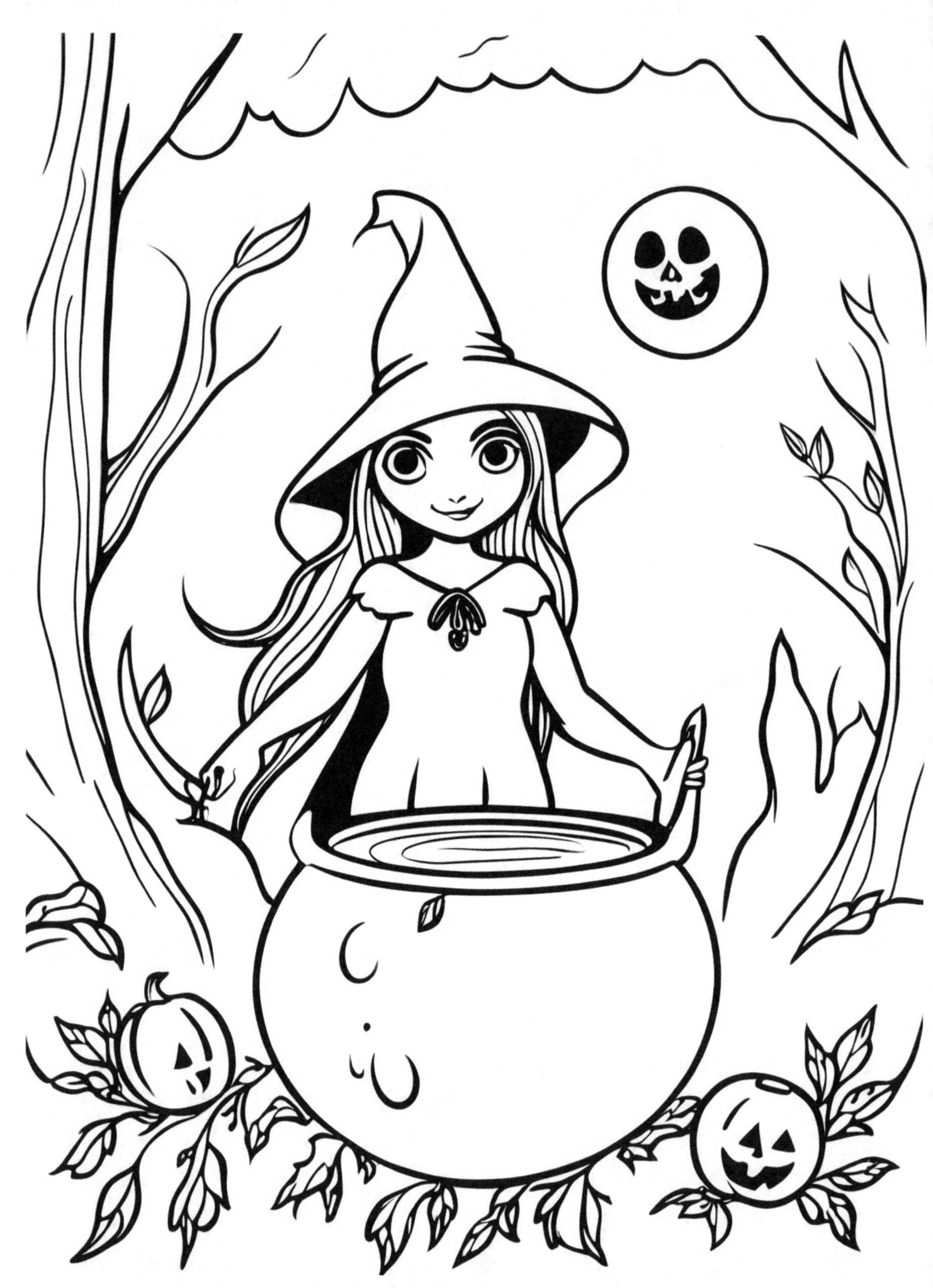

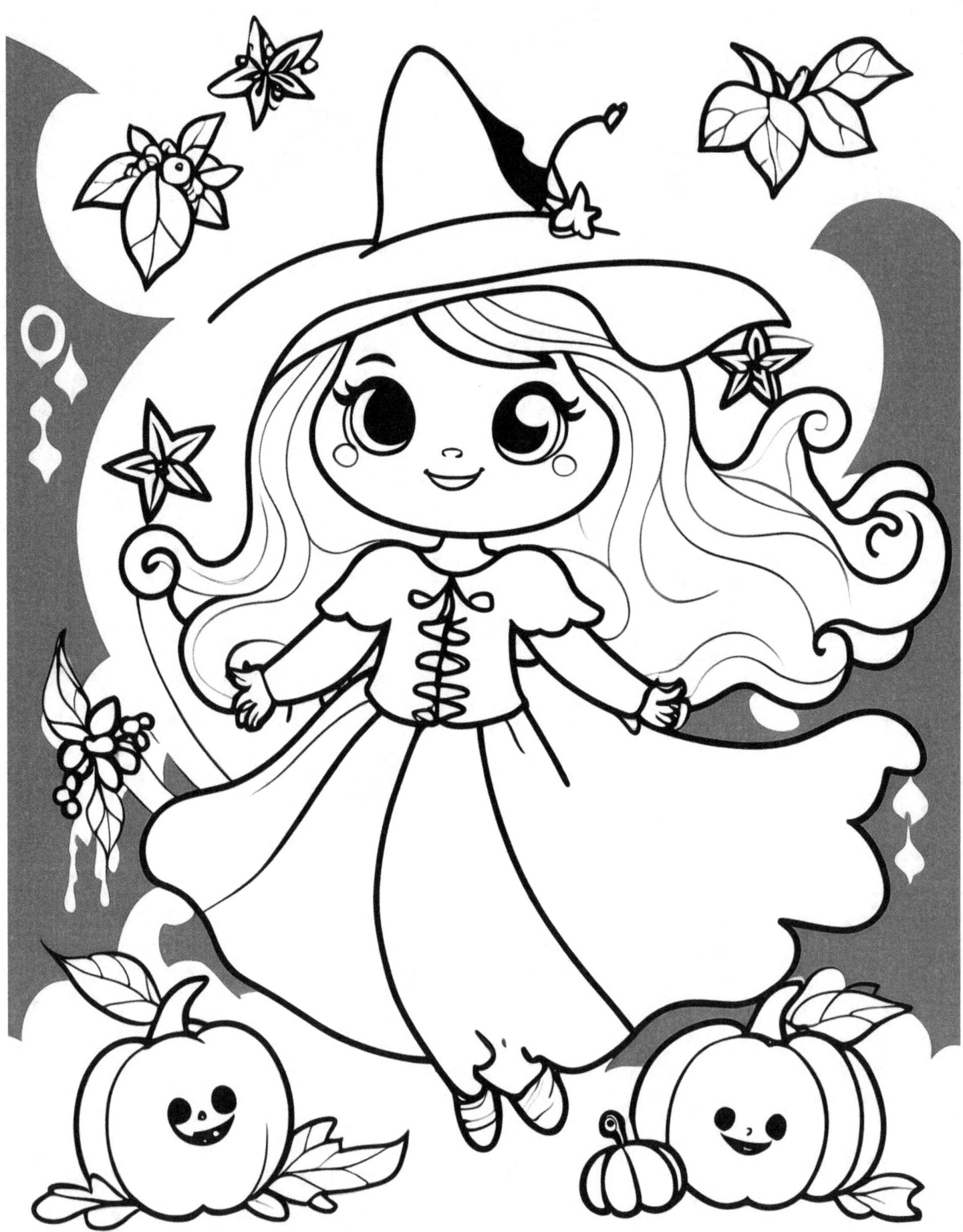

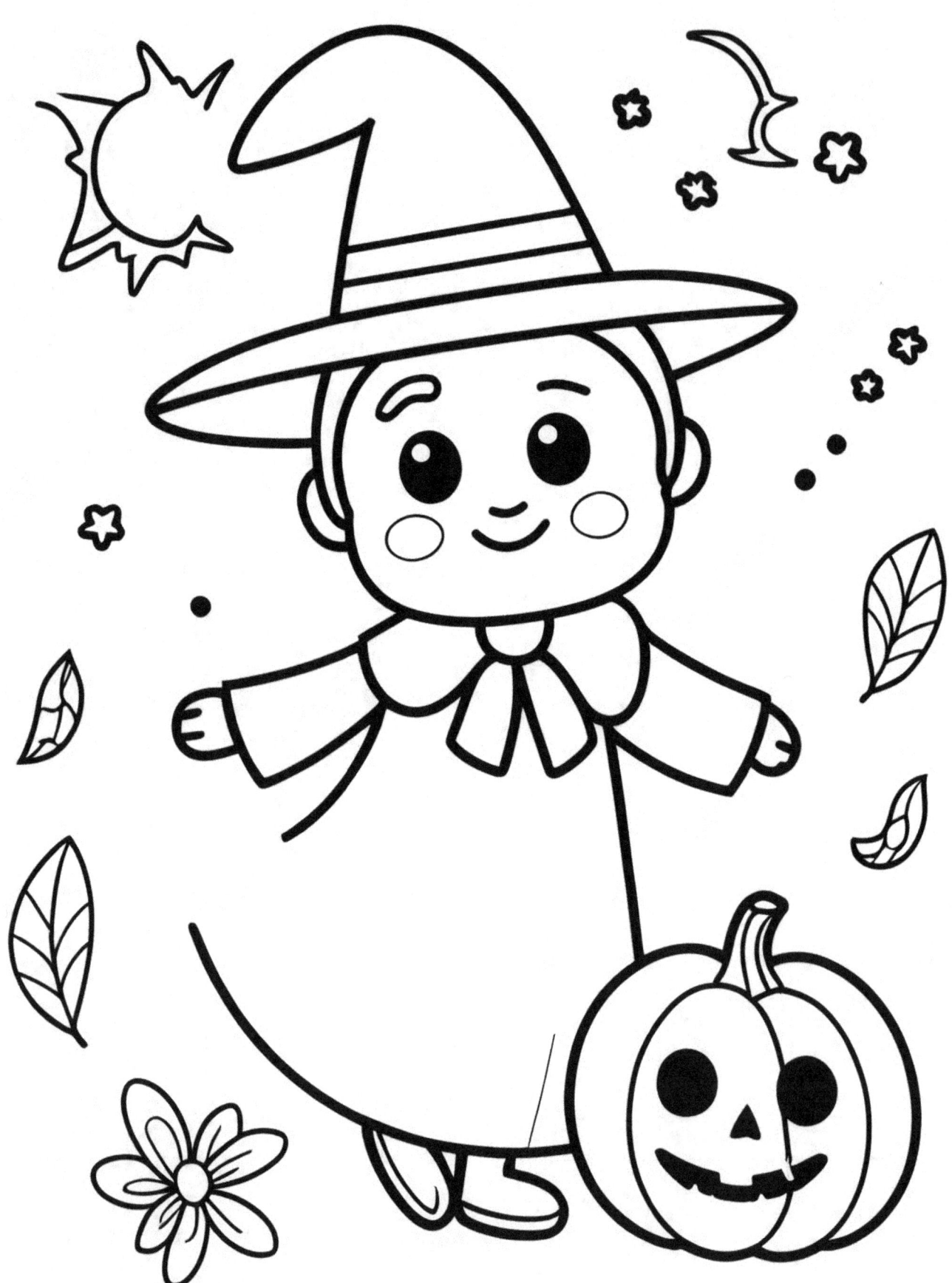

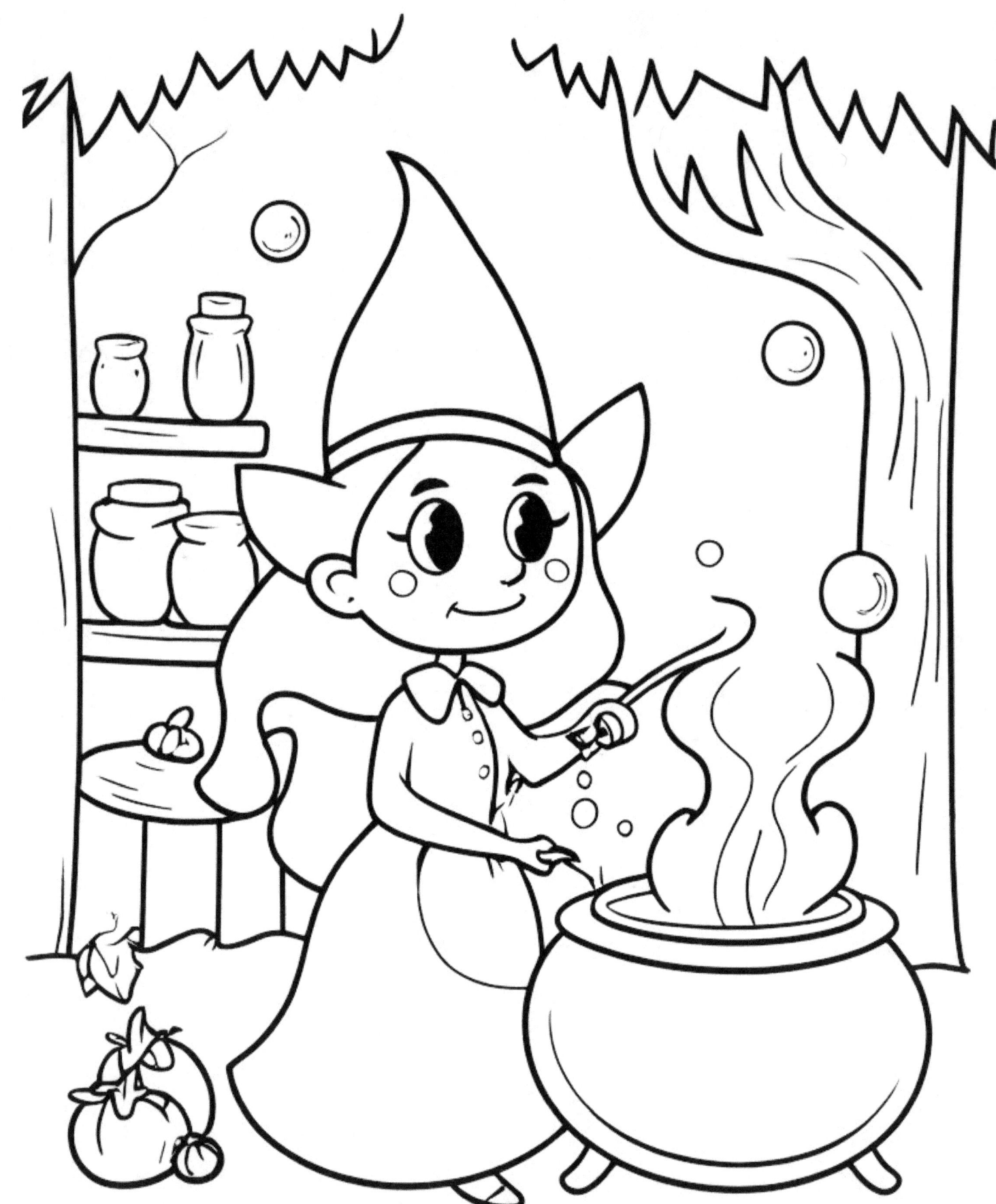

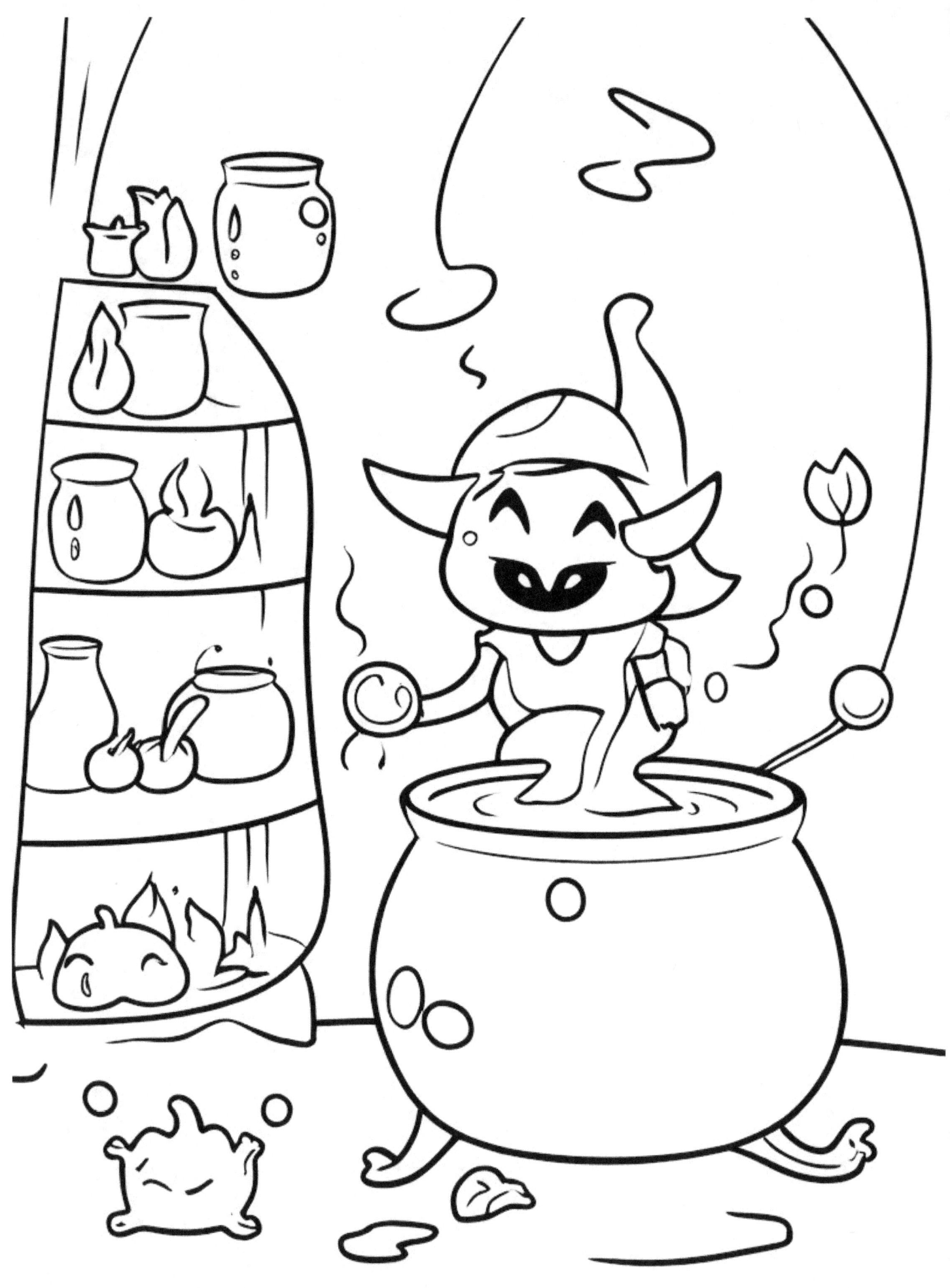

www.ingramcontent.com/pod-product-compliance
Lightning Source LLC
Chambersburg PA
CBHW062113220526
45471CB00010B/3715